# SSAT & ISEE (Lower/Middle) Vocabulary 2000

By

James Shaw

# Copyright Notice

# Introduction

This book is focused on improving your vocabulary and contains over 2000 words that frequently appear in the SSAT Elementary/Middle and ISEE Lower/Middle Examination.

All important question types relevant to the Exam (e.g. Synonyms/ Analogies /Blanks /Double Blanks) are covered to provide adequate practice.

There are 50 sets containing 20 questions each.
**Each set should be done in 10 minutes.**

**Before you begin to take the tests, please note the following points;**

Since the SSAT/ISEE tests are timed, you should practice taking these tests under the time limit of 10 minutes.

Carefully note the instructions for each section. You can easily lose points if you mistake a synonym for an antonym.

For the *'synonym'* questions, think of a word, phrase or definition closest in meaning to the stem word. Then, look for that word or a similar word, among the answer choices.

For the *'sentence completion'* type of questions, if you are unsure, you can plug in the choices one by one to see if the sentence makes logical sense. This strategy often helps eliminate the more obviously wrong choices and lets you focus on fewer relevant choices.

# Test 1

## A. Synonyms

Select the word that most closely matches the meaning of the word provided.

1. OBLIQUE     direct     parallel     level     straight     indirect

2. IMPLICATE     complicate     clarify     incriminate     exonerate     divert

3. PLIABLE     rigid     firm     flexible     brittle     placid

4. SOVEREIGN     subject     ruler     peer     servant     equal

5. FORTHRIGHT     honest     devious     complicated     confused     elusive

## B. Fill in the Blanks

Fill in the blanks from the words in the table below. There is one extra word you do not need.

| disclose | recuperate | legible | synopsis | jubilation | coercion |
|----------|------------|---------|----------|------------|----------|

1. I need to _____ my health after being sick for so long.

2. Please make sure your handwriting is _____, so I can understand what you wrote.

3. There was _____ in the crowd when their favorite team won the match.

4. It is important to _____ any information that could be harmful or sensitive.

5. The _____ of the book is a brief summary of the main events and plot.

## C. Antonyms

| 1. | ANIMOSITY | love | enthusiasm | apathy | indifference | aggression |
|----|-----------|------|------------|--------|--------------|------------|
| 2. | SEVERED | joined | unification | disconnect | separation | dissolution |
| 3. | VIGOR | weakness | strength | energy | vitality | verve |
| 4. | SUPPLEMENT | add | complement | increase | decrease | amplify |
| 5. | HUMILITY | arrogance | modesty | meekness | shyness | submissiveness |

## D. Homophones and Homographs

Homophones are two or more words having the same pronunciation but different spellings and meanings. Homographs are words which have the same spelling but different meanings.

From the list below, fill in the blanks.

| reign | flower | rain | mail | flour |
|-------|--------|------|------|-------|

1. My favorite _____ is a rose.

2. The original fort was built during the _____ of King David I.

3. I received a letter in the _____ today.

4. I use _____ to make bread.

5. The clouds burst, and it started to _____.

# Test 2

## A. Synonyms

Select the word that most closely matches the meaning of the word provided.

|   |   |   |   |   |   |   |
|---|---|---|---|---|---|---|
| 1. | CREDULOUS | skeptical | trusting | cynical | delusional | articulate |
| 2. | TREPIDATION | fear | bravery | excitement | confidence | boredom |
| 3. | OBSERVATION | participation | ignorance | speculation | attention | seeing |
| 4. | FANATIC | enthusiast | hater | moderate | indifferent | fantastic |
| 5. | ARTICULATE | inarticulate | simple | clear | confused | elaborate |

## B. Sentence Completion - Double Blanks

Select the correct answer from the options provided.

1. The cat's _____ fur made it look like it had been in a fight, but it was just _____ after playing with a ball of yarn.

A) well-groomed...tired     B) unkempt...energetic     C) sleek...calm     D) fluffy...sad

2. Sarah was feeling _____ after being stuck in traffic for hours, and her _____ behavior showed it.

A) calm...friendly          B) content...aggressive     C) frustrated...irritable     D) nervous...serene

3. The robbers were known for their _____ when committing their crimes, and the police were worried about how dangerous they could be during a _____.

A) niceness...bank heist     B) ferocity...carjacking     C) lethargy...theft     D) politeness...burglary

4. The new students at the school were _____ when they saw how big the campus was, but they were also _____ about making new friends.

A) excited...worried          B) calm...curious          C) nervous...confident     D) bored...annoyed

## C. Analogies

Select the correct answer from the options provided.

1   LUNGS are to OXYGEN as
A)   heart is to circulation
B)   apple is to pear
C)   car is to plane
D)   tree is to cat
E)   cloud is to rock

2   BED is to SLEEP as
A)   tomato is to banana
B)   dog is to shoe
C)   hammer is to nail
D)   desk is to work
E)   fork is to a spoon

3   PEN is to WRITING as
A)   book is to television
B)   cat is to dog
C)   house is to car
D)   pencil is to marker
E)   key is to unlocking

4   PHONE is to COMMUNICATION as
A)   telephone is to computer
B)   tree is to leaf
C)   book is to knowledge
D)   chair is to table
E)   hammer is to screwdriver

## D. Similar Words - Odd One Out
Mark the word that is NOT similar to the other words.

| | | | | | |
|---|---|---|---|---|---|
| 1. | propitiate | appease | anger | conciliate | placate |
| 2. | cynic | skeptic | pessimist | optimist | misanthrope |
| 3. | zeal | fervor | apathy | enthusiasm | passion |
| 4. | elicit | draw out | extract | suppress | invoke |
| 5. | decline | accept | reject | refuse | repudiate |
| 6. | bewildered | confused | clear | perplexed | lost |
| 7. | genuine | authentic | real | legitimate | fake |

# Test 3

## A. Synonyms

Select the word that most closely matches the meaning of the word provided.

1. VERBOSE      talkative      quiet      shy      brief      rude

2. ZEALOT      fanatic      skeptic      critic      doubter      jealous

3. UTOPIA      hell      average      typical      paradise      mundane

4. TRANSIENT      feeling      temporary      lasting      permanent      stable

5. AFFRONT      insult      compliment      praise      flattery      appreciation

## B. Fill in the Blanks

Fill in the blanks from the words in the table below. There is one extra word you do not need.

| sustain | abide | mirth | toxic | vindictive | upright |
|---------|-------|-------|-------|------------|---------|

1. The spilled chemical was _____ and posed a danger to anyone who came into contact with it.

2. The plant was able to _____ itself for weeks without water because of its deep root system.

3. The dog stood _____ on its hind legs and begged for a treat.

4. The teacher asked the students to _____ by the school's rules while on campus.

5. His _____ behavior towards his former friend surprised everyone who knew him.

## C. Antonyms

Pick the word that means the opposite or near opposite of the word provided.

| | | | | | |
|---|---|---|---|---|---|
| 1. | ALOOF | reserved | unfriendly | frosty | close | hot |
| 2. | BETRAY | abandonment | attack | neglect | uphold | hindrance |
| 3. | DEFICIT | scarcity | surplus | deficiency | need | starvation |
| 4. | WITHHOLD | inflexibility | resolve | avowal | provide | contention |
| 5. | THRIVE | flourish | prosper | grow | succeed | wither |

## D. Homophones and Homographs

Homophones are two or more words having the same pronunciation but different spellings and meanings. Homographs are words which have the same spelling but different meanings.

From the list below, fill in the blanks.

| cell | bare | bear | sell | cel |
|---|---|---|---|---|

1. She could hardly _____ the weight of the heavy suitcase.

2. I can't _____ to watch horror movies because they give me nightmares.

3. I need to charge my _____ phone before it runs out of battery.

4. The look is straight from the anime cartoon, with gorgeous _____ -shaded graphics.

5. I am trying to _____ my old car so that I can buy a newer model.

# Test 4

## A. Synonyms

Select the word that most closely matches the meaning of the word provided.

1. RECKLESS     safe     careful     brave     timid     irresponsible

2. NEMESIS     friend     enemy     affiliate     spouse     ally

3. ABRASIVE     rough     smooth     gentle     sharp     dull

4. BEREFT     happy     ecstatic     angry     lonely     content

5. PARCH     soak     dry out     moisten     hydrate     drown

## B. Sentence Completion - Double Blanks

Select the correct answer from the options provided.

1. The detective _____ that the signed contract was a _____ and began to investigate.

A) modern...fashioned     B) eating...mindful     C) suspected...forgery     D) pillage...astronomical

2. The _____ employee was always the first to _____ for extra shifts.

A) eager...volunteer     B) modern...fashioned     C) lazy...flight     D) running...slowly

3. The _____ shelter was set up to house the people _____ by the fire.

A) temporary...displaced     B) old...new     C) crowd...slowly     D) consuming...caution

4. The city was thrown into _____ after the protest turned _____.

A) bushes...trees     B) ashes...smoke     C) drinking...mindful     D) chaos...violent

## C. Analogies

Select the correct answer from the options provided.

1   SAUNTER is to STROLL as
A)   sprint is to run
B)   hammer is to pillow
C)   pencil is to banana
D)   spleen is to immune system
E)   apple is to pear

2   HURRICANE is to STORM as
A)   book is to television
B)   terrible is to grime
C)   tornado is to whirlwind
D)   fork is to spoon
E)   mammal is to reptile

3   PERCEIVE is to OVERLOOK as
A)   proton is to quark
B)   damage is to danger
C)   rhombus is to square
D)   planet is to the solar system
E)   discern is to miss

4   A SPRINTER is to SPEED as
A)   school is to café
B)   unfruitful is to sanitize
C)   mitochondrion is to cell
D)   marathon runner is to endurance
E)   dog is to squirrel

## D. Similar Words - Odd One Out
Mark the word that is NOT similar to the other words.

| 1. | deserted | abandoned | rescued | rejected | left |
| 2. | grant | bestow | give | provide | deprive |
| 3. | enthrall | captivate | repel | fascinate | charm |
| 4. | naive | cunning | crafty | foxy | wily |
| 5. | inadvertent | consider | ponder | contemplate | deliberate |
| 6. | abominable | divine | vile | contemptable | despicable |
| 7. | gloomy | upbeat | hopeful | bright | cheery |

# Test 5

## A. Synonyms

Select the word that most closely matches the meaning of the word provided.

| | | | | | |
|---|---|---|---|---|---|
| 1. | UPFRONT | honest | devious | shady | sneaky | underhand |
| 2. | TRIVIAL | serious | insignificant | prominent | feeling | significant |
| 3. | PIONEER | trailblazer | followers | indigenous | traditionalist | imitator |
| 4. | ABET | encourage | hinder | daunt | falter | oppose |
| 5. | BIGOT | tolerant | open-minded | intolerant | shouldering | pleasant |

## B. Fill in the Blanks

Fill in the blanks from the words in the table below. There is one extra word you do not need.

| ghastly | biased | distinguished | glade | bounty | aroma |
|---|---|---|---|---|---|

1. The _____ of the freshly baked bread filled the room.

2. It was one of the most _____ crimes ever committed.

3. The judge was accused of being _____ in his decision making.

4. The _____ hunter was known for his success in capturing fugitives and collecting large rewards.

5. The professor's _____ reputation in the academic community was well-deserved, as he had made numerous significant contributions to his field of study.

## C. Antonyms

Pick the word that means the opposite or near opposite of the word provided.

| | | | | | |
|---|---|---|---|---|---|
| 1. | HOSTILITY | enmity | hate | amity | conflict | malice |
| 2. | FLATTER | heaved | butter up | constrained | fawn | belittle |
| 3. | PLIANT | yielding | endorsed | lasting | reasonable | durable |
| 4. | IMMACULATE | pure | ratified | soiled | unsullied | disallowed |
| 5. | LEGITIMATE | coronet | authorized | illicit | kosher | solstice |

## D. Homophones and Homographs

Homophones are two or more words having the same pronunciation but different spellings and meanings. Homographs are words which have the same spelling but different meanings.

From the list below, fill in the blanks.

| dye | die | barking | rode | road |
|---|---|---|---|---|

1.  The doctor said that he was on the _____ to a full recovery.

2.  The dog started _____ when the intruder tried to get into the house at night.

3.  I want to _____ my hair pink for the summer.

4.  When he _____ on horseback for the first time, he was a little scared.

5.  The plant is going to _____ if it doesn't get watered soon.

# Test 6

## A. Synonyms

Select the word that most closely matches the meaning of the word provided.

| 1. | LETHAL | mortal | healthy | dismayed | upend | harmless |
| 2. | MELLOW | uptight | harsh | dulcet | sour | hard |
| 3. | OBLIGE | deject | upset | jangly | dishearten | compel |
| 4. | OMIT | overlook | carry out | incorporate | heed | focus |
| 5. | ABSTAIN | indulge | decomposing | fragile | chafing | shun |

## B. Sentence Completion - Double Blanks

Select the correct answer from the options provided.

1. The airplane had to make a/an _____ landing due to engine _____ .

A) exception...drive      B) studious...flying      C) emergency...failure      D) calm...noise

2. The beautiful _____ of the building hid the crumbling infrastructure _____ it.

A) garden...under      B) facade...beneath      C) roof...stopping      D) door...underneath

3. She was _____ to start her new job, but was disappointed when it turned out to be a _____ position.

A) suspicious...crowd      B) overwhelmed...big      C) sad...new      D) eager...temporary

4. The lights in the theater went out suddenly due to a/an _____ power_____ .

A) unexpected...malfunction      B) sudden...stop      C) quick...brake      D) turn...sharp

## C. Analogies

Select the correct answer from the options provided.

1   WHISPER is to SHOUT as
A)   dicot is to virus
B)   brain is to muscle
C)   sarcastic is to strict
D)   murmur is to scream
E)   trunk is to leaf

2   SWIMMING is to WATER as
A)   beautiful is to grungy
B)   skiing is to snow
C)   tomato is to cucumber
D)   cabin is to tower
E)   tasteless is to scrumptious

3   MOUNTAIN is to HILL as
A)   skyscraper is to house
B)   sunset is to rainbow
C)   run is to evade
D)   flower is to root
E)   dynasty is to roof

4   LONELINESS is to ISOLATION as
A)   hope is to despair
B)   abundance is to scarcity
C)   moral is to rich
D)   ignorance is to prejudice
E)   cashew is to peanut

## D. Similar Words - Odd One Out
Mark the word that is NOT similar to the other words.

| 1. | abrupt | unexpected | gradual | sudden | unforeseen |
|---|---|---|---|---|---|
| 2. | logical | incoherent | articulate | lucid | coherent |
| 3. | open | ajar | agape | unbolted | shut |
| 4. | delayed | overdue | punctual | tardy | slow |
| 5. | disgrace | dignity | honor | decency | splendor |
| 6. | reveal | state | repress | flaunt | declare |
| 7. | definitive | convincing | pivotal | conclusive | hesitant |

# Test 7

## A. Synonyms

Select the word that most closely matches the meaning of the word provided.

| | | | | | |
|---|---|---|---|---|---|
| 1. | GLAMOROUS | appalling | dull | awful | alluring | dowdy |
| 2. | HOSTILE | adverse | amicable | cordial | agreeable | pleasant |
| 3. | IMPEACH | discharge | absolve | forgive | acquit | incriminate |
| 4. | ADOLESCENT | ancient | grown-up | mature | juvenile | adult |
| 5. | TRANQUIL | noisy | agitated | placid | wild | anxious |

## B. Fill in the Blanks

Fill in the blanks from the words in the table below. There is one extra word you do not need.

| flicker | trauma | pungent | aligned | prune | vacant |
|---|---|---|---|---|---|

1. The _____ smell of rotten eggs filled the room, making it difficult to breathe.

2. The light bulb started to _____ before eventually going out completely.

3. After the car accident, the victim experienced _____, which required therapy to heal.

4. The parking lot was totally _____ with not a single car in sight.

5. The two lines on the page were not _____, causing difficulty in reading the text.

## C. Antonyms

Pick the word that means the opposite or near opposite of the word provided.

| | | | | | |
|---|---|---|---|---|---|
| 1. | PRUNE | dapper | snip | add | anguish | cut back |
| 2. | RAMPAGE | riot | calm | anger | tear | rave |
| 3. | SERVILE | slavish | abject | subservient | assertive | obsequious |
| 4. | TEDIOUS | humdrum | bland | stimulating | insipid | wearisome |
| 5. | UNCANNY | bizarre | unearthly | spooky | eerie | normal |

## D. Homophones and Homographs

Homophones are two or more words having the same pronunciation but different spellings and meanings. Homographs are words which have the same spelling but different meanings.

From the list below, fill in the blanks.

| sail | hair | claque | hare | clack |
|---|---|---|---|---|

1. The audience was filled with a _____ of paid supporters.

2. The _____ darted through the field, quickly moving out of sight.

3. The sound of the _____ of the old typewriter filled the room.

4. I need to get my _____ cut before it gets too long.

5. The hard-blowing wind tore the _____ from the boat.

# Test 8

## A. Synonyms

Select the word that most closely matches the meaning of the word provided.

1. UNDERGO     execute     commit     abscond     cut and run     endure

2. VERSATILE     static     limited     adaptable     inflexible     ingenuous

3. SUBLIME     lofty     lowly     mediocre     shabby     lousy

4. RELUCTANT     eager     keen     ready     averse     willing

5. ABHOR     relish     loathe     cherish     approve     desire

## B. Sentence Completion - Double Blanks

Select the correct answer from the options provided.

1. The _____ of the forest was disrupted by the sudden _____ of the hunter.

A) noise...disappearance     B) eager...effort     C) peace...appearance     D) chaos...emergence

2. The _____ of the mountain range was breathtaking, but the _____ of the hike was exhausting.

A) landscape...ease     B) appearance...view     C) time...scenery     D) view...duration

3. Despite his _____ to speak in front of a large crowd, the young boy ultimately gave a/an _____ speech at the school assembly.

A) reluctance...eloquent     B) anxiety...awkward     C) hesitation...nervous     D) stopping...careful

4. The _____ of the performers was impressive, and the _____ of the music was equally mesmerizing.

A) talent...dissonance     B) skill...melody     C) expertise...noise     D) power...beauty

## C. Analogies

Select the correct answer from the options provided.

1  MUSICIAN is to GUITAR as
A)  browsing is to internet
B)  tuna is to salmon
C)  cake is to custard
D)  search is to destroy
E)  painter is to canvas

2  LIGHT SWITCH is to LIGHT as
A)  faucet is to water
B)  seatbelt is to video game
C)  cold is to shiver
D)  gooseberry is to currant
E)  spoon is to chopstick

3  KINDNESS is to COMPASSION as
A)  humility is to arrogance
B)  mountain is to valley
C)  honesty is to integrity
D)  stapler is to pen
E)  refrigerator is to stove

4  LION is to FELINE as
A)  chair is to art
B)  toothbrush is to hygiene
C)  ladder is to sports
D)  crocodile is to reptile
E)  calculator is to gardening

## D. Similar Words - Odd One Out
Mark the word that is NOT similar to the other words.

| | | | | | |
|---|---|---|---|---|---|
| 1. | risk | chance | danger | save | gamble |
| 2. | pessimism | aspiration | distrust | despair | doubt |
| 3. | virtuous | unprincipled | dishonest | devious | corrupt |
| 4. | perpetual | intact | fragmented | continuous | enduring |
| 5. | extravagant | meager | luxurious | opulent | sumptuous |
| 6. | maniac | loony | lunatic | feral | judicious |
| 7. | facile | superficial | facetious | tactful | shallow |

# Test 9

## A. Synonyms

Select the word that most closely matches the meaning of the word provided.

1. AUTHORITATIVE    vulnerable    feeble    minor    lesser    commanding

2. BRAWL    concede    fracas    accord    agreement    compromise

3. LASSITUDE    listlessness    energy    buoyance    vigor    dilution

4. MALFUNCTION    function    gizmo    operate    impairment    contrivance

5. METAPHOR    authenticity    comparison    genuineness    certainty    truth

## B. Fill in the Blanks

Fill in the blanks from the words in the table below. There is one extra word you do not need.

| abolish | collude | blossom | chorus | thriving | malicious |
|---------|---------|---------|--------|----------|-----------|

1. The small business has been _____ since it opened its doors last year.

2. The government voted to _____ the outdated law.

3. The hacker's actions were deemed _____ as they intentionally caused damage to the computer system.

4. The crowd sang in _____ during the national anthem at the sporting event.

5. The rose bush in the garden began to _____ after the rain.

## C. Antonyms

Pick the word that means the opposite or near opposite of the word provided.

| | | | | | |
|---|---|---|---|---|---|
| 1. | COMMODITY | goods | ware | item | junk | product |
| 2. | ACCUMULATE | disperse | pile up | accrue | hoard | collect |
| 3. | ANTIDOTE | cure | antitoxin | venom | medicine | remedy |
| 4. | CALLOW | youth | puerility | facade | nescience | experienced |
| 5. | MISCHIEVOUS | impish | benign | wicked | playful | naughty |

## D. Homophones and Homographs

Homophones are two or more words having the same pronunciation but different spellings and meanings. Homographs are words which have the same spelling but different meanings.

From the list below, fill in the blanks.

| knight | meet | look | night | meat |
|---|---|---|---|---|

1. I took a quick _____ in the mirror to check my appearance.

2. The _____ rode his horse into battle, his armor glinting in the sunlight.

3. The lion devoured the dear, savoring the rich, flavorful _____

4. I always sleep better at _____ when the room is cool and dark.

5. They had the opportunity to _____ the president at a fundraising event.

# Test 10

## A. Synonyms

Select the word that most closely matches the meaning of the word provided.

| | | | | | |
|---|---|---|---|---|---|
| 1. | NOMAD | powerless | wanderer | traditionalist | dictator | skeptic |
| 2. | ORTHODOX | traditional | unconventional | revolutionary | irregular | shady |
| 3. | SARCASTIC | benevolent | polite | gracious | respectful | ironic |
| 4. | VULNERABLE | cautious | secure | exposed | guarded | protected |
| 5. | TYRANT | democrat | reasonable | benefactor | commoner | dictator |

## B. Sentence Completion - Double Blanks

Select the correct answer from the options provided.

1. When traveling to a new place, it is important to _____ local customs and _____.

A) ignore...rules          B) challenge...norms          C) respect...laws          D) overlook...codes

2. The _____ of the performance was excellent, but the _____ of the seats left much to be desired.

A) artistry...comfort          B) talent...performance          C) quality...sight          D) view...site

3. Although it may be tempting to take a shortcut, it is crucial to _____ the guidelines and _____ safety measures.

A) break... compromise          B) challenge...disregard          C) ignore...neglect          D) follow...prioritize

4. Despite her _____ to try new things, the young girl ultimately had a _____ time at the amusement park.

A) reluctance...thrilling          B) enthusiasm...great          C) reluctance...scary          D) skill...delightful

## C. Analogies

Select the correct answer from the options provided.

1  COURAGE is to BRAVERY as
A) music is to literature
B) cowardice is to timidity
C) mountain is to color
D) athleticism is to clumsiness
E) enthusiasm is to apathy

2  ENHANCE is to DIMINISH as
A) improve is to worsen
B) malleability is to flexibility
C) steering wheel is to car
D) learning is to illiteracy
E) famine is to starvation

3  EMINENT is to RENOWNED as
A) pistachio is to an almond
B) obscure is to unknown
C) pebble is to rock
D) milk is to soda
E) day is to month

4  CAT is to MEOW as
A) tiger is to chirp
B) cricket is to bark
C) whale is to song
D) sheep is to roar
E) swallow is to moo

## D. Similar Words - Odd One Out
Mark the word that is NOT similar to the other words.

| 1. | frigid | harsh | uncaring | ardent | unfriendly |
| 2. | ordinance | rule | principle | precept | violation |
| 3. | circumspect | heedless | unaware | oblivious | insensible |
| 4. | aware | mindful | ignorant | conscious | heedful |
| 5. | commoner | compeer | counterpart | fellow | colleague |
| 6. | thrive | flourish | succeed | burgeon | backfire |
| 7. | righteous | notorious | prestigious | meritorious | virtuous |

# Test 11

## A. Synonyms

Select the word that most closely matches the meaning of the word provided.

| | | | | | |
|---|---|---|---|---|---|
| 1. | RESILIENCE | fragility | rigidity | flexibility | weakness | frailty |
| 2. | ABSURDITY | accuracy | farthest | sagacity | rationality | folly |
| 3. | BOLSTER | strengthen | perspicacity | obstruct | discourage | idiocy |
| 4. | CLANDESTINE | public | void | covert | endow | overt |
| 5. | VOCIFEROUS | embolden | noisy | hushed | consolidate | quiet |

## B. Fill in the Blanks

Fill in the blanks from the words in the table below. There is one extra word you do not need.

| berth | disparity | chameleon | encroach | crude | dabble |
|---|---|---|---|---|---|

1. The small boat was docked at the outermost _____ of the marina.

2. The _____ was able to change its skin color to blend in with its surroundings.

3. There was a noticeable _____ between the wealth of the two neighborhoods.

4. The new development was starting to _____ on the wildlife preserve.

5. She likes to _____ in a little bit of everything, but she never fully commits to any one hobby or activity.

## C. Antonyms

Pick the word that means the opposite or near opposite of the word provided.

| | | | | | |
|---|---|---|---|---|---|
| 1. | CULT | religion | sect | fashion | fad | disbelief |
| 2. | BLANDISH | flatter | wheedle | belittle | sweet-talk | cajole |
| 3. | ABROGATE | nullify | revoke | repeal | retract | introduce |
| 4. | CONFER | locality | parley | withhold | confabulate | converse |
| 5. | DAWDLE | crypt | linger | status quo | dart | loiter |

## D. Homophones and Homographs

Homophones are two or more words having the same pronunciation but different spellings and meanings. Homographs are words which have the same spelling but different meanings.

From the list below, fill in the blanks.

| compliment | complement | batter | seeds | cede |
|---|---|---|---|---|

1. The blue curtains were the perfect _____ to the yellow walls in the living room.

2. The _____ hit a home run, much to the delight of the crowd.

3. I was so impressed with the meal that I couldn't help but _____ the chef on their excellent cooking.

4. The country was forced to _____ control of its territory to the invading army.

5. I need to plant the _____ in the garden

# Test 12

## A. Synonyms

Select the word that most closely matches the meaning of the word provided.

| | | | | | | |
|---|---|---|---|---|---|---|
| 1. | CONTEMPTIBLE | ignoble | honorable | bully | exalted | coax |
| 2. | DELIRIOUS | convince | sane | dissuade | balanced | frantic |
| 3. | DISMAYED | aghast | startle | pleased | mollify | delighted |
| 4. | EXPUNGE | palliate | fabricate | form | excise | incense |
| 5. | FLABBERGAST | astonish | sedate | lullaby | drowse | swoop |

## B. Sentence Completion - Double Blanks

Select the correct answer from the options provided.

1. The best way to avoid getting lost while traveling is to _____ a map and _____ your location.

A) follow...hide          B) ignore...location          C) follow...mark          D) overlook...codes

2. The food at the restaurant was _____, but the service was _____.

A) presentation...speed          B) delicious...slow          C) quality...location          D) comfort...proximity

3. The cool breeze _____ her hair and made her feel more alert and _____.

A) ruffled...energetic          B) neat...calm          C) soft...lively          D) smooth...tranquil

4. James was feeling _____ after receiving a good grade on his test, and his _____ behavior showed it.

A) calm...uncouth          B) excited...exuberant          C) enthused...rude          D) happy...impolite

## C. Analogies

Select the correct answer from the options provided.

1   UNITED STATES is to NORTH AMERICA as
A)  Germany is to South America
B)  rainbow is to cloud
C)  hand is to foot
D)  sentence is to paragraph
E)  tissue is to skeleton

2   NILE is to EGYPT as
A)  Mississippi river is to USA
B)  basement is to garden
C)  Earth is to milky way
D)  trees are to pond
E)  hurricane is to tornado

3   SCULPTING is to CLAY as
A)  baking is to canvas
B)  breach is to endanger
C)  dolphin is to click
D)  sleep is to fatigue
E)  fishing is to rod

4   PROSE is to NOVELIST as
A)  blazing is to gardener
B)  diplomacy is to war
C)  woodwork is to carpenter
D)  invisible is to ransack
E)  pounce is to run

## D. Similar Words - Odd One Out
Mark the word that is NOT similar to the other words.

| | | | | | |
|---|---|---|---|---|---|
| 1. | startle | disconcert | certainty | frighten | shock |
| 2. | ineptitude | knack | incapacity | inability | silliness |
| 3. | flawless | paragon | model | bizarre | exemplar |
| 4. | selfsame | analogous | tantamount | indistinguishable | diverse |
| 5. | daunt | motivate | excite | encourage | stimulate |
| 6. | fundamental | negligible | trivial | minor | unimportant |
| 7. | cynicism | distrust | skepticism | assurance | uncertainty |

# Test 13

## A. Synonyms

Select the word that most closely matches the meaning of the word provided.

1. WICKED     virtuous     iniquitous     harmless     moral     pacifist

2. TRANSLUCENT     opaque     vague     loud     diaphanous     thick

3. SULLEN     amiable     jocund     smug     merry     gloomy

4. APPREHEND     confound     misconstrue     grasp     obfuscate     obscure

5. ADHERE     loosen     cling     detach     let go     apart

## B. Fill in the Blanks

Fill in the blanks from the words in the table below. There is one extra word you do not need.

| aesthetic | figurative | equilibrium | declare | facilitate | grovel |
|---|---|---|---|---|---|

1. In order to achieve a state of _____, it is imperative to find a balance between opposing forces.

2. The new software is designed to _____ communication between team members by providing a platform for collaboration.

3. She used a/an _____ expression to describe the situation, saying that it was "a storm in a teacup."

4. He was willing to _____ and beg for forgiveness in order to repair the damage to their relationship.

5. The _____ appeal of the art gallery was enhanced by the careful placement of each piece.

## C. Antonyms

Pick the word that means the opposite or near opposite of the word provided.

| | | | | | |
|---|---|---|---|---|---|
| 1. | AGHAST | shocked | stunned | unafraid | astonished | dumbfounded |
| 2. | ANOMALY | oddity | normality | peculiarity | abnormality | irregularity |
| 3. | BEQUEST | dispossess | inheritance | legacy | heritage | estate |
| 4. | CONTRIVED | artificial | authentic | forced | necessary | unnatural |
| 5. | DILIGENT | assiduous | obligatory | earnest | attentive | lazy |

## D. Homophones and Homographs

Homophones are two or more words having the same pronunciation but different spellings and meanings. Homographs are words which have the same spelling but different meanings.

From the list below, fill in the blanks.

| auricle | peace | oracle | sentence | piece |
|---|---|---|---|---|

1. The _____ treaty ended the long and bloody war between the two countries.

2. The _____ is the small, curved outer part of the ear.

3. I need to find a _____ of paper to write down this phone number.

4. He was serving a two year _____ for fraud.

5. The ancient Greeks believed that the _____ at Delphi had the power to see the future.

# Test 14

## A. Synonyms

Select the word that most closely matches the meaning of the word provided.

1. ABATE     intensify     expand     enhance     necessitated     diminish

2. BELLICOSE     pacifist     mild     belligerent     assortment     gracious

3. CAPITULATE     conquer     withstand     resist     succumb     fight

4. DEBUNK     discredit     fabrication     agree     support     uphold

5. EPOCH     timeless     instant     era     literature     moment

## B. Sentence Completion - Double Blanks

Select the correct answer from the options provided.

1. _____ is an important step in the _____ of medicines, helping to eliminate unwanted material.

A) purification...synthesis     B) combination...fusion     C) gather...interaction     D) fusion...separation

2. His _____ attitude allowed him to pass all of his exams with _____ colors.

A) bad...good     B) negative...bright     C) positive...flying     D) optimistic...top

3. The _____ of a volcano is a result of molten rock, or magma, rising to the _____.

A) eruption...surface     B) top...deepness     C) explosion...deep     D) release...crust

4. Gravity is a good example of _____ at a _____.

A) power...combination     B) intensity...power     C) distance...strength     D) force...distance

## C. Analogies

Select the correct answer from the options provided.

1   PINNACLE is to HEIGHT as
A)   page is to report
B)   shoulders are to waist
C)   astronomical is to minimal
D)   abyss is to depth
E)   portable is to movable

2   PHOTOSYNTHESIS is to PLANT as
A)   destroy is to generate
B)   flying is to bird
C)   nurse is to infirmary
D)   circus is to perform
E)   gallery is to athlete

3   TAXONOMY is to CLASSIFICATION as
A)   brick is to carton
B)   sand is to drinking
C)   smoldering is to iodine
D)   pencil is to marker
E)   hierarchy is to order

4   PLOW is to FARMER as
A)   scalpel is to surgeon
B)   practice is to water
C)   green is to data
D)   curtain is to physician
E)   pane is to registrar

## D. Similar Words - Odd One Out
Mark the word that is NOT similar to the other words.

| | | | | | |
|---|---|---|---|---|---|
| 1. | sluggish | inert | diligent | idle | slow |
| 2. | insignificance | pride | self-respect | nobility | honor |
| 3. | halt | flourish | decrease | collapse | dwindle |
| 4. | apathy | dislike | zest | lethargy | disinterest |
| 5. | cause | pacify | provoke | make | prompt |
| 6. | jiggle | be still | shake | wriggle | joggle |
| 7. | perplex | baffle | confuse | elucidate | flummox |

# Test 15

## A. Synonyms

Select the word that most closely matches the meaning of the word provided.

| | | | | | |
|---|---|---|---|---|---|
| 1. | MAYHEM | turmoil | acumen | burnish | concurrence | harmony |
| 2. | JUXTAPOSED | distant | cajole | contrasted | discrete | boon |
| 3. | LACKLUSTER | feigned | enormity | brilliant | drab | vivid |
| 4. | GIMMICK | frugal | honesty | cognizant | frankness | ploy |
| 5. | EXASPERATE | infuriate | placate | iconoclast | soothe | delight |

## B. Fill in the Blanks

Fill in the blanks from the words in the table below. There is one extra word you do not need.

| predominant | arouse | acoustics | rebuke | adage | quart |
|---|---|---|---|---|---|

1. The _____ of the room was designed to enhance the sound quality for concerts.

2. She poured a _____ of milk into the pot before making the pudding.

3. The supervisor delivered a stern _____ to the workers for coming in late to work.

4. The _____ color in the artwork is a deep blue, which draws the viewer's attention immediately.

5. Many people believe that the _____ "honesty is the best policy" is a wise principle to follow in life.

## C. Antonyms

Pick the word that means the opposite or near opposite of the word provided.

| | | | | | |
|---|---|---|---|---|---|
| 1. | AMOROUS | dispassionate | loving | fond | adoring | affectionate |
| 2. | BOLSTER | soothe | beguile | undermine | obdurate | support |
| 3. | WRITHE | twist | be still | defunct | wriggle | aggrandize |
| 4. | VITRIOLIC | bitter | knell | rancorous | neophyte | kind |
| 5. | TEPID | lukewarm | halfhearted | toady | enthusiastic | laconic |

## D. Homophones and Homographs

Homophones are two or more words having the same pronunciation but different spellings and meanings. Homographs are words which have the same spelling but different meanings.

From the list below, fill in the blanks.

| choirs | quires | lune | loon | palm |
|---|---|---|---|---|

1.    The package contained two _____ of tracing paper.

2.    The _____ sang beautiful hymns during the church service.

3.    The _____'s distinctive call echoed across the lake.

4.    He held the bird gently in the _____ of his hand.

5.    The _____ is a crescent-shaped curve or area, often used in geometry or astronomy.

# Test 16

## A. Synonyms

Select the word that most closely matches the meaning of the word provided.

1. DEMAGOGUE    listener    agitator    appeaser    gauge    incumbent

2. COUNTERFEIT    phony    delightful    disseminate    promulgate    genuine

3. BARRICADE    cordon    entrance    solipsism    phlegmatic    flabbergast

4. ANTIQUITY    modernity    travesty    yesteryear    recalcitrant    contemporary

5. QUEASY    construe    dazing    ubiquitous    satisfied    nauseous

## B. Sentence Completion - Double Blanks

Select the correct answer from the options provided.

1. In order to conserve energy and reduce our carbon footprint, it's crucial to be _____ with our use of _____.

A) aware...fan      B) mindful...electricity      C) conscious...wood      D) reckless...tools

2. His _____ attitude towards life allowed him to overcome adversity and achieve _____ success.

A) focused...noteworthy      B) ambitious...nothing      C) rash...huge      D) apathetic...great

3. The _____ store was known for its unique selection of _____ home decor items.

A) retro...resale      B) book...antique      C) archaic...new      D) vintage...handcrafted

4. The _____ from the summit was beautiful, but the steep trek to get there was _____.

A) sight...passage      B) view...challenging      C) scene...fun      D) position...descent

## C. Analogies

Select the correct answer from the options provided.

1    PERISH is to DIE as
A)   water is to suggest
B)   thrive is to flourish
C)   profound is to tentative
D)   occasional is to suggest
E)   impolite is to distinct

2    HONESTY is to INTEGRITY as
A)   deceit is to duplicity
B)   valiant is to vacillate
C)   doubtful is to convincing
D)   paltry is to intermittent
E)   sporadic is to horizontal

3    GARDENING is to PLANTS as
A)   competent is to prosper
B)   profitable is to whimsical
C)   farming is to crops
D)   frighten is to cherry
E)   atmosphere is to metal

4    ATHLETE is to BASKETBALL as
A)   breathe is to nitrogen
B)   ring is to phone call
C)   student is to hospital
D)   office is to worker
E)   musician is to guitar

## D. Similar Words - Odd One Out
Mark the word that is NOT similar to the other words.

| | | | | | |
|---|---|---|---|---|---|
| 1. | frugal | economical | extravagant | sparing | parsimonious |
| 2. | extension | sprawl | spread | shrink | stretch |
| 3. | apostate | loyalist | deserter | turncoat | traitor |
| 4. | adroit | dexterous | incompetent | adept | proficient |
| 5. | ruin | ravage | raze | create | destroy |
| 6. | frolic | romp | page-turner | potboiler | bore |
| 7. | expert | novice | specialist | old hand | veteran |

# Test 17

## A. Synonym

Select the word that most closely matches the meaning of the word provided.

1. ABDICATE     resume     yoke     tirade     renounce     remain

2. BELIE     confirm     contradict     prove     reveal     ratify

3. CANARD     truth     wader     false report     grove     verity

4. DEFUNCT     obsolete     alive     modern     existing     up to date

5. EXUBERANCE     apathy     enthusiasm     factualness     beater     indifference

## B. Fill in the Blanks

Fill in the blanks from the words in the table below. There is one extra word you do not need.

| brusque | amiss | consolidate | refutation | anecdote | scathing |
|---------|-------|-------------|------------|----------|----------|

1. The senator's _____ of the president's speech was met with cheers from the audience.

2. The CEO's _____ attitude made him very unpopular.

3. The detective could tell something was _____ as soon as he arrived at the crime scene.

4. The journalist's _____ review of the new restaurant left many people wondering if they should bother trying it out.

5. The company's new marketing campaign was designed to _____ its position in the international market.

## C. Antonyms

Pick the word that means the opposite or near opposite of the word provided.

| 1. | ACCEDE | grant | reject | palliate | colonel | agree |
| 2. | ASININE | foolish | obfuscate | fetter | silly | clever |
| 3. | CHRONIC | enduring | abjure | fleeting | bereft | lingering |
| 4. | GRANDIOSE | smooth talk | modest | bashful | exaggerated | lavish |
| 5. | JOLLITY | gaiety | seriousness | eclectic | impractical | joviality |

## D. Homophones and Homographs

Homophones are two or more words having the same pronunciation but different spellings and meanings. Homographs are words which have the same spelling but different meanings.

From the list below, fill in the blanks.

| through | reseed | recede | drop | threw |
|---|---|---|---|---|

1. The difficult questions in the test _____ me off.

2. The water level in the lake began to _____ as the drought continued.

3. The restaurant has suffered a big _____ in trade.

4. The boy waded _____ the water to reach his boat.

5. Some plants _____ themselves indefinitely.

# Test 18

## A. Synonyms

Select the word that most closely matches the meaning of the word provided.

1. EXTOL    deprecate    eulogize    virtuoso    denounce    slapdash

2. FOMENT    dampen    unrestrained    wanton    reduce    stimulate

3. GAUNT    venerate    thin    plump    upbraid    chubby

4. INGRESS    exit    zephyr    access    choir    exodus

5. INTREPID    rapid    cowardly    flurry    craven    courageous

## B. Sentence Completion - Double Blanks

Select the correct answer from the options provided.

1. In order to stay healthy, it's crucial to be _____ of the food we eat and the water we drink, and to be _____ about germs and maintaining cleanliness.

A) mindful...cautious    B) careless...aware    C) alert...precise    D) conscious...willful

2. She had a/an _____ approach to her studies, which helped her earn _____ grades.

A) good...focused    B) ambitious...minor    C) determined...high    D) impressive...fewer

3. The _____ market was filled with a variety of _____ items, from furniture to collectibles.

A) flea...painting    B) antique...fashioned    C) thrift...old    D) secondhand...new

4. The _____ of the city skyline was impressive, but the marathon _____ was grueling.

A) walk...show    B) colors...line    C) scent...running    D) view...race

## C. Analogies

Select the correct answer from the options provided.

1   VULGAR is to DECENT as
A)   immoral is to upright
B)   tree is to forest
C)   water is to wind
D)   holiness is to durable
E)   eccentric is to peculiar

2   YOLK is to EGG as
A)   carp is to fish
B)   hat is to pant
C)   pit is to cherry
D)   pillow is to feet
E)   peace is to buddies

3   HUNGER is to APPETITE as
A)   doctor is to sick
B)   fever is to infection
C)   lonesome is to happy
D)   defame is to esteem
E)   friend is to animosity

4   PERSISTENCE is to DETERMINATION as
A)   shyness is to timidity
B)   snag is to rip
C)   agreeable is to splendor
D)   skilled is to green
E)   innocuous is to malicious

## D. Similar Words - Odd One Out
Mark the word that is NOT similar to the other words.

| | | | | | |
|---|---|---|---|---|---|
| 1. | plush | sumptuous | substandard | high-class | luxurious |
| 2. | taunt | sneer | compliment | dig | jibe |
| 3. | gentle | curt | gruff | abrupt | harsh |
| 4. | flurry | burst | bustle | tranquil | flood |
| 5. | unwilling | submissive | acquiescent | consenting | yielding |
| 6. | amalgamate | integrate | fuse | separate | mingle |
| 7. | entreat | beseech | demand | plead | implore |

# Test 19

## A. Synonyms

Select the word that most closely matches the meaning of the word provided.

1. INSURMOUNTABLE    easy      paradigm      insuperable      peninsula      unproblematic

2. LACKADAISICAL    isthmus      energetic      apathetic      chorus      strenuous

3. ARBITRATOR    laconic      provoker      judge      maelstrom      audience

4. LIAISON    disintegrate      sheep      link      maverick      disconnection

5. INNUMERABLE    few      incalculable      robust      syrupy      finite

## B. Fill in the Blanks

Fill in the blanks from the words in the table below. There is one extra word you do not need.

| despite | ample | sermon | passionate | retribution | unscathed |
|---------|-------|--------|------------|-------------|-----------|

1. The young man was seeking _____ for the wrongs done to him.

2. The pastor delivered a powerful _____ that moved many in the congregation to tears.

3. Despite the ordeal, the survivor emerged _____, having suffered no physical harm.

4. There was _____ evidence to support the defendant's innocence.

5. The _____ fan could not contain their excitement for the upcoming concert.

## C. Antonyms

Pick the word that means the opposite or near opposite of the word provided.

1.  AUSPICIOUS    opportune    ominous    propitious    glutton    spartan

2.  IMPRUDENCE    dense    quirky    genius    unanimous    dull

3.  CIRCUMSPECT    reckless    libelous    cautious    deferential    prudent

4.  DOWNTRODDEN    subjugated    respected    catnap    salutation    oppressed

5.  FORLORN    cheerful    lost    latch    pitiful    malign

## D. Homophones and Homographs

Homophones are two or more words having the same pronunciation but different spellings and meanings. Homographs are words which have the same spelling but different meanings.

From the list below, fill in the blanks.

| bark | bail | bale | assistance | assistant |
|------|------|------|------------|-----------|

1.  The accused criminal posted _____ to secure his release from jail.

2.  The farmer wrapped the hay into a tight _____ for storage.

3.  Teachers can't give pupils any _____ in exams.

4.  The _____ of the juniper tree is very hard.

5.  The _____ took the book and checked the price on the back cover.

# Test 20

## A. Synonyms

Select the word that most closely matches the meaning of the word provided.

| | | | | | |
|---|---|---|---|---|---|
| 1. | IMPOVERISHED | allege | distinctive | affluent | penurious | wealthy |
| 2. | HAUGHTY | arrogant | meek | humble | bind | unbridle |
| 3. | JEST | fortuity | advise | joke | killjoy | catastrophe |
| 4. | PERIPHERAL | central | succor | antagonism | minor | focal |
| 5. | RICKETY | wobbly | stable | dismay | entice | firm |

## B. Sentence Completion - Double Blanks

Select the correct answer from the options provided.

1. _____ is a valuable skill to have, but it's crucial to also _____ safety precautions when using tools.

A) cooking...overlook    B) woodworking...follow    C) gardening...flout    D) painting...ignore

2. After the hurricane hit, they were only able to _____ a few of their belongings from their _____ home.

A) rescue...flooded    B) recover...dirty    C) save...scorched    D) repair...new

3. The _____ of the canyon was stunning, but the _____ of the rappelling was intimidating.

A) vision...wandering    B) scene...walking    C) view...descent    D) sight...travelling

4. To prevent illness, it's important to be _____ about what we touch and to be _____ about washing our hands.

A) conscious...unaware    B) mindful...ignorant    C) aware...forgetful    D) careful...diligent

## C. Analogies

Select the correct answer from the options provided.

| | | | |
|---|---|---|---|
| 1 | TRICKLE is to STREAM as | 2 | SHOPPING is to STORES as |
| A) | strange is to denigrate | A) | lavatory is to experiment |
| B) | bitter is to pleasant | B) | browsing is to internet |
| C) | cordial is to frosty | C) | labyrinth is to classroom |
| D) | sports are to sweeping | D) | biology is to tutorial |
| E) | push is to shove | E) | museum is to painting |
| | | | |
| 3 | APPEASE is to ANGER as | 4 | SWIPE is to CARD as |
| A) | book is to television | A) | computer is to keyboard |
| B) | cat is to dog | B) | tube is to toothpaste |
| C) | house is to car | C) | dribble is to basketball |
| D) | pacify is to violence | D) | broom is to sweep |
| E) | key is to opening | E) | soldier is to war |

## D. Similar Words - Odd One Out
Mark the word that is NOT similar to the other words.

| | | | | | |
|---|---|---|---|---|---|
| 1. | murky | filthy | sterile | muddy | soiled |
| 2. | commendable | contemptible | contemptuous | vile | disgraceful |
| 3. | swanky | stylish | sassy | obsolete | chic |
| 4. | low | downhearted | despondent | gleeful | glum |
| 5. | crevice | fissure | solid | crack | cleft |
| 6. | offensive | allowance | forbidden | proscribed | prohibited |
| 7. | mysterious | apparent | cryptic | esoteric | mystifying |

# Test 21

## A. Synonyms

Select the word that most closely matches the meaning of the word provided.

| | | | | | |
|---|---|---|---|---|---|
| 1. | DEBAUCHERY | dexterity | depravity | probity | coronation | goodness |
| 2. | COMMEMORATE | flout | concoction | honor | essential | ignore |
| 3. | INDETERMINATE | indefinite | hoax | recognized | furtive | acknowledged |
| 4. | VICTORIOUS | stony | triumphant | vex | vanquished | whitewashed |
| 5. | SUBTLETY | discrepancy | cuisine | delicacy | bad behavior | fluency |

## B. Fill in the Blanks

Fill in the blanks from the words in the table below. There is one extra word you do not need.

| drizzle | baleful | entourage | craven | discreet | portentous |
|---|---|---|---|---|---|

1.  The politician was surrounded by a/an _____ of supporters as he made his way through the crowd.

2. A thin _____ of rain fell from the sky, dampening the ground.

3. The King was criticized for his _____ decision to flee rather than stay and fight.

4.  The school bully hated me and usually gave me a _____ look.

5.  The _____ speech by the corrupt dictator sent ripples of uncertainty through the population.

## C. Antonyms

Pick the word that means the opposite or near opposite of the word provided.

1. KINDLE     ignite     douse     torpid     brisk     spark

2. IRREFUTABLE     unassailable     futile     disputable     astute     certain

3. HISTRIONIC     staged     theatrical     historic     restrained     dramatic

4. EXTROVERTED     sociable     cordial     convivial     quixotic     shy

5. FLAMBOYANT     flashy     telepathic     clairvoyant     quiet     showy

## D. Homophones and Homographs

Homophones are two or more words having the same pronunciation but different spellings and meanings. Homographs are words which have the same spelling but different meanings.

From the list below, fill in the blanks.

| colonel | patients | patience | kernel | well |
|---------|----------|----------|--------|------|

1. The _____ is the edible part of a grain, seed, or fruit.

2. Making small-scale models takes a great deal of _____.

3. The _____ commanded a unit of soldiers in the war.

4. Tina has performed _____ in the exam.

5. _____ are waiting longer to see a consultant.

# Test 22

## A. Synonyms

Select the word that most closely matches the meaning of the word provided.

| | | | | | | |
|---|---|---|---|---|---|---|
| 1. | DEFIANCE | obedience | submission | insolence | vicissitude | compliance |
| 2. | CONSCIENTIOUS | rushed | injudicious | diligent | imprudent | offhand |
| 3. | AWRY | repeated | crooked | straight | on course | impromptu |
| 4. | INTENSIFIED | abated | repeated | faded | deepened | diminished |
| 5. | MAGNANIMOUS | trivial | benevolent | troublesome | petty | niggling |

## B. Sentence Completion - Double Blanks

Select the correct answer from the options provided.

1. The firefighters were able to _____ several people from the burning _____, but unfortunately, some were unable to be rescued.

A) retrieve...terrible     B) rescue...building     C) gather...wood     D) deteriorate...road

2. _____ is a great way to stay active and healthy, but it's vital to _____ the proper safety equipment.

A) swimming...forget     B) skateboarding...avoid     C) driving...overlook     D) cycling...wear

3. In order to maintain good health, it's important to be _____ about what we eat and to be _____ about the ingredients in our food.

A) careful...knowledgeable     B) reckless...familiar     C) alert...accustomed     D) watchful...unfamiliar

4. We must rest assured that our sorrows, if any, are short-lived and a period of joy _____ us. Such thinking will always maintain our _____ and peace of mind.

A) befits...body     B) awaits...equipoise     C) begets...dream     D) bemoans...skills

## C. Analogies

Select the correct answer from the options provided.

1  DRESS is to FABRIC as
A) horrid is to hideous
B) handle is to sword
C) chair is to wood
D) seed is to sapling
E) gravel is to glass

2  ICE CREAM is to CHOCOLATE CHIPS as
A) citrus is to leaf
B) axe is to lumberjack
C) college is to learning
D) face is to makeup
E) demolish is to mend

3  CHEMISTRY is to ELEMENTS as
A) psychology is to behaviors
B) philosophy is to design
C) literature is to music
D) civics is to calibrations
E) accounting is to words

4  CALLOUSNESS is to INSENSITIVITY as
A) forget is to remember
B) water is to blaze
C) building is to architecture
D) rational is to absurd
E) empathy is to compassion

## D. Similar Words - Odd One Out
Mark the word that is NOT similar to the other words.

| | | | | | |
|---|---|---|---|---|---|
| 1. | pivot | twirl | whirl | stationary | rotate |
| 2. | nippy | glacial | chilly | frosty | scalding |
| 3. | benevolence | callousness | compassion | commiseration | tenderness |
| 4. | concurrently | instantaneously | consecutively | in chorus | simultaneously |
| 5. | slack | limp | taut | floppy | loose |
| 6. | jubilant | thwarted | proud | euphoric | thrilled |
| 7. | modest | diffident | bashful | bold | reserved |

# Test 23

## A. Synonyms

Select the word that most closely matches the meaning of the word provided.

| | | | | | |
|---|---|---|---|---|---|
| 1. | EFFERVESCENT | static | nirvana | fizzy | valediction | at a halt |
| 2. | PULVERIZE | crush | construct | alias | inaugurated | manufacture |
| 3. | REMUNERATION | debt | hurtle | payment | tarry | cost |
| 4. | SCRUPULOUS | meticulous | careless | batten | impound | sloppy |
| 5. | UPHOLSTERY | nitpicking | padding | baring | vetoing | emptying |

## B. Fill in the Blanks

Fill in the blanks from the words in the table below. There is one extra word you do not need.

| tactician | parsimonious | squabbling | pompous | vivid | vandal |
|---|---|---|---|---|---|

1. The two sides were unable to come to an agreement and ended up _____ for hours over the issue.

2. The young man was known to be a _____, frequently breaking into buildings and defacing property.

3. The _____ was able to come up with a clever plan to outmaneuver their opponents on the battlefield.

4. The _____ businessman was always looking for ways to save money, even if it meant cutting corners on important expenses.

5. The CEO's _____ behavior made him unpopular with his employees, who found him difficult to work with.

## C. Antonyms

Pick the word that means the opposite or near opposite of the word provided.

| | | | | | |
|---|---|---|---|---|---|
| 1. | PLIANT | malleable | beguile | hypnotize | stiff | supple |
| 2. | AROMATIC | fragrant | odorless | enervate | firebrand | scented |
| 3. | METICULOUS | scrupulous | thorough | squelch | promulgate | negligent |
| 4. | LAUDATORY | assuage | sycophantic | damning | congratulatory | moderation |
| 5. | HEREDITARY | synchronized | genetic | acquired | heterogeneous | transmitted |

## D. Homophones and Homographs

Homophones are two or more words having the same pronunciation but different spellings and meanings. Homographs are words which have the same spelling but different meanings.

From the list below, fill in the blanks.

| council | ring | counsel | gorilla | guerrilla |
|---|---|---|---|---|

1. My sister gave me a beautiful _____ for my birthday.

2. The _____ met to discuss important issues affecting the community.

3. The _____ is the strongest of the anthropoid animals.

4. I sought _____ from a trusted advisor before making a major decision.

5. The _____ fighter used unconventional tactics to fight against the enemy.

# Test 24

## A. Synonyms

Select the word that most closely matches the meaning of the word provided.

1. CHARISMATIC    repellent    tenet    captivating    rejuvenate    repulsive

2. AUDACIOUS    craven    nomenclature    autonomous    daring    timorous

3. BEDLAM    iconoclast    tranquility    serendipity    stability    mayhem

4. DESULTORY    methodical    impetus    precise    aimless    thoughtful

5. LAMPOON    parody    support    frail    imperative    admire

## B. Sentence Completion - Double Blanks

Select the correct answer from the options provided.

1. The divers were able to _____ several artifacts from the sunken _____, but they had to be careful not to damage them.

A) find...destroyed      B) retrieve...vessel      C) collect...ruin      D) leave...ship

2. Professionals focus their _____ on fulfilling their responsibilities and achieving results, not on _____ a particular image.

A) energies...portraying      B) abilities... interposing    C) planning...devising      D) skills...obtaining

3. It's important to stay active and get regular exercise to maintain good _____ and to prevent _____ diseases like heart disease and diabetes.

A) fitness...infectious      B) strength...illness      C) energy...ailment      D) health...chronic

4. In order to be successful in school, it's important to be organized and _____ your time wisely. This will help you to _____ on your studies and avoid getting overwhelmed.

A) ignore...procrastinate      B) manage...focus      C) waste...concentrate    D) handle...fall behind

## C. Analogies

Select the correct answer from the options provided.

1 APPROVAL is to ACCEPTANCE as
A) sanctity is to profanity
B) expletive is to blessing
C) domain is to giddiness
D) disloyalty is to fidelity
E) rejection is to denial

2 CONFIDENCE is to SELF-ASSURANCE as
A) doctrine is to grateful
B) scruple is to certainty
C) agitation is to composure
D) indecisiveness is to uncertainty
E) immense is to infinitesimal

3 SCYTHE is to RANCHER as
A) chisel is to sculptor
B) cash is to monkey
C) reaper is to shopkeeper
D) granary is to food
E) sickle is to police

4 THESAURUS is to DICTIONARY as
A) apple is to core
B) almanac is to calendar
C) poet is to sonnet
D) music is to rap
E) talk is to converse

## D. Similar Words - Odd One Out
Mark the word that is NOT similar to the other words.

| 1. | gape | ignore | stare | ogle | gawk |
| 2. | separation | segregation | integration | exclusion | setting apart |
| 3. | spontaneous | premeditated | thought-out | deliberate | intentional |
| 4. | commend | extol | reprimand | hail | flatter |
| 5. | zenith | nadir | foot | bottom | base |
| 6. | babble | blather | belt up | chatter | jabber |
| 7. | capitulate | resist | surrender | cede | yield |

# Test 25

## A. Synonyms

Select the word that most closely matches the meaning of the word provided.

| | | | | | |
|---|---|---|---|---|---|
| 1. | ABYSMAL | appalling | superlative | lunar | stellar | consent |
| 2. | BELLIGERENT | conciliatory | abstinence | consecration | amiable | quarrelsome |
| 3. | CHASTISE | praise | tremor | extol | brewery | rebuke |
| 4. | ERRONEOUS | accurate | particular | specious | brazen | veracious |
| 5. | LUMINESCENCE | dullness | imperishability | brevity | glow | obscurity |

## B. Fill in the Blanks

Fill in the blanks from the words in the table below. There is one extra word you do not need.

| implored | depleted | autonomous | hawser | coalesce | accentuate |
|----------|----------|------------|--------|----------|------------|

1.  The company's board of directors _____ the CEO to come up with a plan to save the failing business.

2.  The artist used dark colors to _____ the sadness in the painting.

3.  The water droplets _____ together to form a puddle.

4.  The town's resources were _____ due to the drought.

5.  His ship was tied to the dock with a thick _____.

## C. Antonyms

Pick the word that means the opposite or near opposite of the word provided.

1. EXHILARATING    stimulating    contemptuous    tedious    elating    philanthropic

2. EBB    fade    surge    anathema    protean    diminish

3. DISCERNIBLE    indistinct    evident    apparent    defibrillator    obvious

4. CONVOLUTED    complex    intricate    simple    strait    tortuous

5. ASSIMILATE    reject    heretical    incorporate    peninsula    integrate

## D. Homophones and Homographs

Homophones are two or more words having the same pronunciation but different spellings and meanings. Homographs are words which have the same spelling but different meanings.

From the list below, fill in the blanks.

| martial | match | marshal | principal | principle |
|---------|-------|---------|-----------|-----------|

1. A federal _____ was killed in a shoot-out.

2. The _____ of the school is responsible for overseeing the administration and management of the institution.

3. If proven, he could face a court _____ and military prison.

4. The _____ of fairness is something that we should all strive to uphold.

5. Whatever your color scheme, there's a fabric to _____.

# Test 26

## A. Synonyms

Select the word that most closely matches the meaning of the word provided.

1.  WINCE        grin          slyness          grimace          ingenuity          smile

2.  VACUOUS      astute        gore             shrewd           plasma             mindless

3.  TRANSPOSE    retain        move             juncture         keep               interval

4.  STIFLE       nurture       disbursement     foster           levies             suppress

5.  RETICENCE    reserve       chattiness       scholarly        imagination        magician

## B. Sentence Completion - Double Blanks

Select the correct answer from the options provided.

1. With large classes, it is difficult for teachers to _____ regular essay-type questions for homework because _____ long answers would take too much time.

A) give...marking          B) pursue...feeling          C) consider...making          D) revalue...concise

2. The _____ of the moon causes the _____ of the ocean's tides.

A) gravity...rise          B) light...drop          C) spin...fall          D) turning...drip

3. The cat _____ into the bushes when it saw the dog _____ towards it.

A) sit...barking          B) race...entering          C) run...ran          D) ran...running

4. The boy _____ the soccer ball into the net, _____ the winning goal.

A) hit...done          B) jolted...made          C) kicked...scoring          D) pushed...reach

## C. Analogies

Select the correct answer from the options provided.

1  GERMINATION is to SEED as
A) piston is to engine
B) incubation is to egg
C) bishop is to church
D) pizza is to bake
E) sprouting is to rock

2  CLIMAX is to PLOT as
A) puzzle is to piece
B) crescendo is to sound
C) wolf is to dog
D) circle is to cube
E) fast is to food

3  LULL is to SLEEP as
A) channel is to sailing
B) cry is to sorrow
C) exercise is to better health
D) hutch is to rabbit
E) abstract is to summary

4  ENRICH is to IMPOVERISH as
A) augment is to decrease
B) coiffure is to hairstyle
C) discount is to reduction
D) egocentric is to selfish
E) perfume is to eternal

## D. Similar Words - Odd One Out
Mark the word that is NOT similar to the other words.

| | | | | | |
|---|---|---|---|---|---|
| 1. | peril | menace | deathtrap | refuge | exposure |
| 2. | assertion | avowal | denial | proclamation | declaration |
| 3. | deface | embellish | adorn | ornament | enhance |
| 4. | stroll | run | saunter | wander | amble |
| 5. | agree | waver | choose | decide | elect |
| 6. | expand | aggrandize | degrade | boost | inflate |
| 7. | rushed | hasty | rapid | deliberate | hurried |

# Test 27

## A. Synonyms

Select the word that most closely matches the meaning of the word provided.

1. RESTITUTION      hauteur        timidity        compensation      occupation      seizure

2. PIED             variegated     fearfulness     analogy           rivalry         plain

3. NAIL             spike          loosen          trim down         expatiate       release

4. INVIGORATED      depleted       revitalized     outspread         concord         fatigued

5. FECUND           barren         temporary       prolific          arid            infertile

## B. Fill in the Blanks

Fill in the blanks from the words in the table below. There is one extra word you do not need.

| bimonthly | gargantuan | fatuous | sympathetic | callous | abscond |
|-----------|------------|---------|-------------|---------|---------|

1. The prisoner managed to _____ from the maximum-security prison by digging a tunnel under the fence.

2. The library holds _____ book club meetings on the first and third Tuesday of every month.

3. The comedian's joke was _____ and not funny at all.

4. The mansion was _____, with at least twenty bedrooms and a pool the size of a small lake.

5. She was shocked by the _____ attitude of the doctor towards the suffering of his patients.

## C. Antonyms

Pick the word that means the opposite or near opposite of the word provided.

| | | | | | |
|---|---|---|---|---|---|
| 1. | EXQUISITE | aggrandize | hideous | didactic | exemplary | refined |
| 2. | DISSONANCE | harmony | travesty | strife | enervate | disunity |
| 3. | CONTRADICTION | ambiguity | solipsism | consistency | incompatibility | ascetic |
| 4. | KEEP | hold | alacrity | remain | retain | shed |
| 5. | SCRUTINIZE | examine | pore over | eclectic | glance | solidarity |

## D. Homophones and Homographs

Homophones are two or more words having the same pronunciation but different spellings and meanings. Homographs are words which have the same spelling but different meanings.

From the list below, fill in the blanks.

| faze | bass | phase | jean | gene |
|---|---|---|---|---|

1. The project is in the final _____ and is expected to be completed soon.

2. The scientists identified a defective _____.

3. Even serious threats did not _____ the opposition leader.

4. She's wearing bell-bottom Levis and a faded _____ jacket.

5. They unloaded their catch of cod and _____.

# Test 28

## A. Synonyms

Select the word that most closely matches the meaning of the word provided.

| | | | | | | |
|---|---|---|---|---|---|---|
| 1. | COWER | stand tall | humdrum | cringe | capricious | fearlessness |
| 2. | ARCHETYPE | imitation | model | contort | clinch | replica |
| 3. | CAMARADERIE | animosity | dismantle | antipathy | enmity | companionship |
| 4. | BASTION | weak spot | pomposity | arrogance | stronghold | deficiency |
| 5. | DELINEATE | conceal | circumspect | hide | chary | define |

## B. Sentence Completion - Double Blanks

Select the correct answer from the options provided.

1. The teacher _____ the students to be on time for class, or they would be _____.

A) reminded...punished    B) lectured...rewarded    C) scolded...paid    D) praised...penalized

2. The singer _____ the stage and began to _____ her new hit song.

A) left...sing    B) entered...flying    C) walked onto...perform    D) ran off...start

3. The cat _____ its tail and _____ away when the dog barked at it.

A) twitched...ran    B) waved...run    C) panicked...slow    D) pulled...fast

4. The counselor was _____ towards her clients, _____ their feelings.

A) emphatic... unfeeling    B) gentle...cold    C) kind...understanding    D) sympathetic...cruel

## C. Analogies

Select the correct answer from the options provided.

1  SUBMARINE is to NAVY as
A) boulevard is driving
B) melt is to liquid
C) bicycle is to highway
D) subway is to public
E) ferry is to school

2  GRAM is to WEIGHT as
A) gallon is to capability
B) cheese is to cheddar
C) stall is to horse
D) infant is to crib
E) meter is to distance

3  SCULPTURE is to MARBLE as
A) window is to curtain
B) pottery is to clay
C) flour is to bread
D) bacon is to beef
E) vocalist is to choir

4  TSUNAMI is to WAVE as
A) happy is to elated
B) parsimonious is to egotistic
C) earthquake is to tremor
D) wind is to hurricane
E) grove is to trees

## D. Similar Words - Odd One Out
Mark the word that is NOT similar to the other words.

| # | | | | |
|---|---|---|---|---|
| 1. | unproductive | unfruitful | thriving | infertile | barren |
| 2. | serious | flip | witty | droll | jesting |
| 3. | shield | armor | buffer | expose | screen |
| 4. | revolting | vile | striking | abhorrent | hideous |
| 5. | inhibition | looseness | autonomy | liberty | openness |
| 6. | peril | liability | welfare | hazard | jeopardy |
| 7. | mocking | reverent | derisive | cynical | scornful |

# Test 29

## A. Synonyms

Select the word that most closely matches the meaning of the word provided.

| | | | | | |
|---|---|---|---|---|---|
| 1. | ACCREDITED | unsanctioned | affability | denied | brusqueness | recognized |
| 2. | BELIE | contradict | validate | perturb | discompose | confirm |
| 3. | CAPRICE | consideration | billow | asphyxiate | whim | caution |
| 4. | EMACIATED | thin | inconsequential | exigent | chubby | plump |
| 5. | FALLIBLE | long-suffering | infallible | imperfect | synthetic | dependable |

## B. Fill in the Blanks

Fill in the blanks from the words in the table below. There is one extra word you do not need.

| imprudent | deleterious | lucid | discreet | egregious | harrowing |
|---|---|---|---|---|---|

1. The _____ effects of pollution on the environment are becoming more and more evident as time goes on.

2. The crime was _____ and warranted a severe punishment.

3. The survivor's story of the _____ disaster brought tears to their eyes.

4. It is generally _____ to make crucial decisions when you are feeling overwhelmed or emotional, as they can often have deleterious consequences.

5. The speaker's explanation was _____ and easy to understand.

## C. Antonyms

Pick the word that means the opposite or near opposite of the word provided.

| 1. | ADEPT | proficient | equanimity | disparate | inept | adroit |
| 2. | EMBARRASSMENT | chagrin | confidence | eccentric | mortification | gratis |
| 3. | DIVERGENT | inveterate | similar | conflicting | insipid | deviating |
| 4. | EXTROVERTED | sociable | diffident | gregarious | woolly | incumbent |
| 5. | INDUCE | persuade | sway | pejorative | discourage | unpretentious |

## D. Homophones and Homographs

Homophones are two or more words having the same pronunciation but different spellings and meanings. Homographs are words which have the same spelling but different meanings.

From the list below, fill in the blanks.

| waive | wave | faint | feinted | cast |
|-------|------|-------|---------|------|

1.  I felt _____ and had to sit down for a moment.

2.  The criminal decided to _____ their right to a trial and pleaded guilty.

3.  The scientist used a machine to demonstrate the principles of _____ motion.

4.  After the accident, my leg was in a _____ for about six weeks.

5.  The boxer _____ a punch to the left, but then delivered a powerful blow to the right.

# Test 30

## A. Synonyms

Select the word that most closely matches the meaning of the word provided.

1. DESPONDENT    optimistic    fairground    hopeless    unconvincing    cheerful

2. GENTEEL    vulgar    manufactured    fictive    crude    refined

3. IMPERIL    protect    be adamant    transfigure    endanger    shield

4. DISTRUSTFUL    suspicious    trusting    unforthcoming    trusting    illustrative

5. DEVIATE    remit    proliferation    power through    diverge    conform

## B. Sentence Completion - Double Blanks

Select the correct answer from the options provided.

1. The school's principal is known for her _____ approach to discipline, and the students' _____ behavior reflects this.

A) good...poor          B) strict...good          C) decent...terrible          D) upright...bad

2. The new restaurant has _____ a lot of attention since it _____ last month.

A) heard...closed          B) grabbed...ban          C) received...opened          D) caught...starting

3. The young artist _____ many awards for her paintings, which have been _____ in galleries all over the country.

A) won...exhibited          B) deserved...exposed          C) lost...shown          D) failed...presented

4. The company _____ a lot of criticism after it was revealed that they had _____ the environment.

A) met...cleaned          B) got...cleansed          C) tackled...purified          D) faced...polluted

## C. Analogies

Select the correct answer from the options provided.

1  FAIRNESS is to JUSTICE as
A)  bias is to discrimination
B)  worker is to boss
C)  lance is to spear
D)  invisible is to perceive
E)  failure is to pleasing

2  TOOL is to TOOLBOX as
A)  balm is to moisture
B)  harbor is to ship
C)  motorcycle is to garage
D)  drawer is to clothes
E)  pen is to paper

3  HIKING is to TRAILS as
A)  painting is to brush
B)  favor is to oppose
C)  driving is to car
D)  acting is to theater
E)  door is to break

4  DROUGHT is to FAMINE as
A)  wallet is to money
B)  inflation is to recession
C)  bread is to sandwich
D)  nap is to sleep
E)  health is to infection

## D. Similar Words - Odd One Out
Mark the word that is NOT similar to the other words.

| | | | | | |
|---|---|---|---|---|---|
| 1. | incredulous | convinced | dubious | wary | skeptical |
| 2. | facilitate | hinder | thwart | impede | delay |
| 3. | general | broad | restricted | all-embracing | extensive |
| 4. | treachery | duplicity | fraudulence | honesty | deceit |
| 5. | soil | contaminate | sully | purify | taint |
| 6. | benefactor | backer | sponsor | patron | foe |
| 7. | altruism | philanthropy | selfishness | benevolence | selflessness |

# Test 31

## A. Synonyms

Select the word that most closely matches the meaning of the word provided.

| | | | | | |
|---|---|---|---|---|---|
| 1. | RIDGE | crest | aerobics | valley | surmise | flat |
| 2. | SHODDY | fine | inferior | remit | code-name | meticulous |
| 3. | TACIT | stated | explicit | borough | farming | implicit |
| 4. | UBIQUITOUS | omnipresent | scarce | sublime | pastoral | rare |
| 5. | ELOQUENCE | unintelligibility | fluency | discreet | inconspicuous | stammering |

## B. Fill in the Blanks

Fill in the blanks from the words in the table below. There is one extra word you do not need.

| vacillate | zealous | ruminate | repay | woeful | sedentary |
|---|---|---|---|---|---|

1. My little brother is _____ about soccer and he practices every day and never wants to miss a game.

2. The dog's _____ expression indicated that it was unhappy.

3. He was known to _____ on important decisions, often causing delays in the project.

4. The _____ lifestyle of the office worker often leads to health problems.

5. After a long day at work, I like to _____ on my accomplishments and think about what I can do to improve the next day.

## C. Antonyms

Pick the word that means the opposite or near opposite of the word provided.

| | | | | | |
|---|---|---|---|---|---|
| 1. | INSOLVENT | bankrupt | mulish | wealthy | stubborn | destitute |
| 2. | IRK | pester | harmonized | varied | delight | vex |
| 3. | MANNERLY | boorish | civil | trivial | colossal | courteous |
| 4. | MIRAGE | figment | reality | chaste | nightmare | immodest |
| 5. | OPULENT | poor | mendacious | literal | affluent | prosperous |

## D. Homophones and Homographs

Homophones are two or more words having the same pronunciation but different spellings and meanings. Homographs are words which have the same spelling but different meanings.

From the list below, fill in the blanks.

| grease | content | Greece | groan | grown |
|---|---|---|---|---|

1. The old door let out a _____ as it was opened.

2. I need to add some _____ to the engine to keep it running smoothly.

3. The tomato plants had _____ tall and produced a bountiful crop.

4. _____ is a country in southern Europe with a rich history and culture.

5. Alan seems fairly _____ with his life.

# Test 32

## A. Synonyms

Select the word that most closely matches the meaning of the word provided.

| | | | | | |
|---|---|---|---|---|---|
| 1. | BYSTANDER | idyll | participant | pastoral | contestant | onlooker |
| 2. | WAFT | trudge | float | husbandry | countrified | strong wind |
| 3. | VEHEMENT | apathetic | passionate | harvester | rupture | indifferent |
| 4. | TIMID | gallant | analytic | shy | synthetic | bold |
| 5. | SNIVEL | cackle | hasten | chuckle | procrastinate | whimper |

## B. Sentence Completion - Double Blanks

Select the correct answer from the options provided.

1. The instructor _____ the pupils to think critically and _____ their own ideas.

A) cast down...create    B) encouraged...develop    C) put off...manage    D) discourage...make

2. The athlete _____ hard to improve her skills and _____ her chances of winning.

A) performed...reduce    B) practiced...enhance    C) did...decrease    D) trained...lessen

3. The new movie has _____ rave reviews since it _____ in theaters last week.

A) gained...opened    B) get...started    C) added...descended    D) many...close

4. The politician _____ a lot of support from voters after his speech, in which he _____ his stance on important issues.

A) received...clarified    B) met...accepted    C) had...disagreed    D) expected...confused

## C. Analogies

Select the correct answer from the options provided.

1   LOCK is to SECURITY as
A) poverty is to prosperity
B) chess is to box
C) door is to bolt
D) microphone is to communicate
E) stairs are to snooze

2   ATOM is to MOLECULE as
A) bottle is to salad
B) coerce is to force
C) house is to kitchen
D) cockpit is to plane
E) album is to song

3   LOBE is to EAR as
A) quiet is to silence
B) market is to park
C) hermit is to recluse
D) pasta is to sauce
E) blade is to propeller

4   CENSURE is to CRITICIZE as
A) adulate is to flatter
B) restitution is to expense
C) progress is to regress
D) jargon is to tactic
E) peasant is to royalty

## D. Similar Words - Odd One Out
Mark the word that is NOT similar to the other words.

| | | | | | |
|---|---|---|---|---|---|
| 1. | abject | dismal | happy | gloomy | wretched |
| 2. | hardship | adversity | affliction | fluke | misfortune |
| 3. | furtive | flagrant | unconcealed | deliberate | blatant |
| 4. | participant | viewer | witness | watcher | observer |
| 5. | contemptuous | critical | approving | hypercritical | censorious |
| 6. | condone | punish | overlook | tolerate | pardon |
| 7. | skill | ineptitude | knack | flair | aptitude |

# Test 33

## A. Synonyms

Select the word that most closely matches the meaning of the word provided.

| | | | | | | |
|---|---|---|---|---|---|---|
| 1. | MALADROIT | clumsy | adlibbed | deft | impulsive | dexterous |
| 2. | NONCOMMITTAL | guarded | definite | audacious | demure | decisive |
| 3. | PERMEABLE | airtight | porous | water-resistant | set off | moratorium |
| 4. | RAVENOUS | stuffed | greedy | transpire | herald | generous |
| 5. | ACUMEN | craziness | sidestep | hopelessness | shrewdness | inability |

## B. Fill in the Blanks

Fill in the blanks from the words in the table below. There is one extra word you do not need.

| latitude | furl | mischievous | obedience | peculiar | dividend |
|---|---|---|---|---|---|

1. The tourist found the local customs _____.

2. The soldiers were taught to show _____ to their commanding officer.

3. The _____ of a place determines how far North or South it is located on the Earth's surface.

4. The sailors _____ the sails when they are not being used to keep them from getting damaged by the wind.

5. Their _____ pranks always meant they had a good time together, although they often ended up in trouble.

## C. Antonyms

Pick the word that means the opposite or near opposite of the word provided.

1. INTERMINABLE    finite      ceaseless      undeviating      svelte      perpetual

2. HALLOWED      profane      pejorative      dubious      consecrated      holy

3. FISSURE      crevice      pertinacious      crack      docile      closing

4. AMASS      unsmiling      smug      accumulate      disperse      accrue

5. PRURIENT      salacious      decent      refractory      subservient      nosy

## D. Homophones and Homographs

Homophones are two or more words having the same pronunciation but different spellings and meanings. Homographs are words which have the same spelling but different meanings.

From the list below, fill in the blanks.

| canon | cannon | affectation | affection | interest |
|-------|--------|-------------|-----------|----------|

1. The couple showed each other _____ with a hug and a kiss.

2. The _____ of classical literature includes works by authors such as Homer, Shakespeare, and Dante.

3. The _____ was a powerful weapon used in warfare during the medieval period.

4. Emily's accent was just a/an _____, not her real way of speaking.

5. Unfortunately, I lost _____ halfway through the film.

# Test 34

## A. Synonyms

Select the word that most closely matches the meaning of the word provided.

| | | | | | |
|---|---|---|---|---|---|
| 1. | VIRULENT | lethal | discord | non-toxic | concord | benign |
| 2. | TORMENT | comfort | flattener | cosmonaut | torture | hilarity |
| 3. | SURREPTITIOUS | overt | scramble | covert | expatiate | open |
| 4. | REPREHENSIBLE | decent | blameworthy | infringe | countermand | praiseworthy |
| 5. | PRECLUDE | impede | bifurcate | permit | expatiate | facilitate |

## B. Sentence Completion - Double Blanks

Select the correct answer from the options provided.

1. The company _____ a new program to _____ the efficiency of their operations.

A) launched...degrade    B) initiated...worsen    C) implemented...improve    D) introduced...fail

2. The team has _____ teamwork skills. They always _____ well to achieve their goals.

A) strong...collaborate    B) weak...cooperate    C) poor...unite    D) bad...band

3. The scientist _____ a lot of research and _____ a groundbreaking new theory.

A) executed...closed    B) performed...shut    C) carried out...maintain    D) conducted...developed

4. She has a _____ sense of fashion. Her outfits are always _____ with style and flair.

A) poor...having    B) great...bursting    C) good...lacking    D) bad...filled

## C. Analogies

Select the correct answer from the options provided.

1  ENCOURAGE is to DISSUADE as
A)  belittle is to disrespect
B)  poverty is to destitution
C)  inspire is to deter
D)  poultry is to chicken
E)  bottle is to cork

2  OLFACTORY is to SMELL as
A)  auditory is to hear
B)  visible is to taste
C)  pungent is to touch
D)  acoustic is to see
E)  echo is to sniff

3  ENVY is to JEALOUSY as
A)  preserve is to destroy
B)  proactive is to dormant
C)  shake is to stillness
D)  quiver is to steady
E)  hope is to optimism

4  KERNEL is to CORN COB as
A)  delicate is to shatter
B)  grain is to rice
C)  records are to dresser
D)  bushes are to brushes
E)  harbor is to ship

## D. Similar Words - Odd One Out
Mark the word that is NOT similar to the other words.

| | | | | | |
|---|---|---|---|---|---|
| 1. | lachrymose | weepy | chirpy | sorrowful | dismal |
| 2. | emancipation | liberation | release | incarceration | deliverance |
| 3. | psychosis | lunacy | folly | lucidity | insanity |
| 4. | disquiet | discontent | optimism | melancholy | malaise |
| 5. | mesmerize | enthrall | bore | rivet | beguile |
| 6. | mollify | enrage | placate | appease | pacify |
| 7. | nebulous | precise | vague | tenuous | hazy |

# Test 35

## A. Synonyms

Select the word that most closely matches the meaning of the word provided.

1. AVARICE      generosity      abhorrence      acrimony      philanthropy      greed

2. CONVALESCENCE      recuperation      decline      diurnal      nocturnal      deterioration

3. DIVULGE      cover      disclose      sojourn      obscure      conceal

4. HEDONIST      ambition      activist      beaver      pleasure seeker      ascetic

5. FOREBODING      ominous      boosting      lifting      holdover      encouraging

## B. Fill in the Blanks

Fill in the blanks from the words in the table below. There is one extra word you do not need.

| regal | criterion | masquerade | enthusiasm | awash | dogmatic |
|-------|-----------|------------|------------|-------|----------|

1. The King's attire was _____, befitting his status.

2. The lawmaker's _____ stance on the issue made it hard for others to agree with him.

3. The school used test scores as a _____ for admission.

4. Their _____ for sports always meant they had a good time together, although they sometimes got injured.

5. The _____ party was filled with mysterious and intriguing guests, all wearing elaborate masks and costumes.

## C. Antonyms

Pick the word that means the opposite or near opposite of the word provided.

| | | | | | |
|---|---|---|---|---|---|
| 1. | LURID | vivid | travesty | whets | dull | garish |
| 2. | GOUGE | fill | vulgar | cut | imprecision | carve |
| 3. | EXCURSION | jaunt | stay | raucous | subdued | trip |
| 4. | TACITURN | introverted | vacillated | reticent | retrospective | communicative |
| 5. | SIESTA | slumber | quinoa | nap | wake | darnel |

## D. Homophones and Homographs

Homophones are two or more words having the same pronunciation but different spellings and meanings. Homographs are words which have the same spelling but different meanings.

From the list below, fill in the blanks.

| cite | site | sight | hour | our |
|---|---|---|---|---|

1. Houses have been built on the periphery of the factory _____.

2. The teacher asked the students to _____ their sources in their research papers.

3. _____ team won the championship game, much to the delight of the fans.

4. If your _____ is poor, you should not drive a car.

5. It will take about a/an _____ to get to the beach from here.

# Test 36

## A. Synonyms

Select the word that most closely matches the meaning of the word provided.

1.  INTRACTABLE   obstinate   manageable   exemption   holiday   easygoing

2.  MALIGNANT   benevolent   take a vacation   be happening   cancerous   gentle

3.  OSTENTATIOUS   modest   sermonize   discreet   converge   showy

4.  IMPEDE   permit   prevent   gaucherie   handiness   bar

5.  SODDEN   arid   incidentals   dry   stipend   soaked

## B. Sentence Completion - Double Blanks

Select the correct answer from the options provided.

1. The artist has a _____ sense of color. His paintings are always _____ with vibrant hues.

A) terrible...lacking        B) bad...having        C) remarkable...packed     D) great...empty

2. Surprisingly, despite the price being very _____, the product was of a _____ quality.

A) less...awful        B) low...superb        C) cheap...bad        D) good...fine

3. Skilled workers improve _____ and _____ of their company and contribute to its growth

A) efficiency...productivity     B) time...success        C) inefficiency...output     D) failure...quality

4. Students who have experienced difficult, frustrating and not very _____ learning environments often end up forming _____ attitudes towards education.

A) enjoyable...gratifying     B) pleasant...confident   C) fun...positive        D) successful...negative

## C. Analogies

Select the correct answer from the options provided.

1  FLY is to HELICOPTER as
A) marble is to spread
B) loom is to fabric
C) hairdresser is to hair
D) chef is to baguette
E) navigate is to ship

2  RESOURCEFULNESS is to CREATIVITY as
A) innovate is to stagnate
B) selfless is to self-centered
C) reality is to fantasy
D) hopscotch is to game
E) punctuality is to reliability

3  WOLF is to LUPINE as
A) fox is to leporine
B) sheep is to ovine
C) rabbit is to crocodilian
D) crocodile is to macropod
E) kangaroo is to vulpine

4  TELESCOPE is to ASTRONOMY as
A) oscilloscope is to physics
B) stethoscope is to meteorology
C) seismograph is to chemistry
D) barometer is to biology
E) thermometer is to psychology

## D. Similar Words - Odd One Out
Mark the word that is NOT similar to the other words.

| | | | | | |
|---|---|---|---|---|---|
| 1. | novelty | innovation | conservatism | freshness | originality |
| 2. | determined | obstinate | persistent | submissive | tenacious |
| 3. | obscure | ambiguous | discernable | abstruse | incomprehensible |
| 4. | speaker | listener | orator | lecturer | raconteur |
| 5. | pang | comfort | twinge | spasm | cramp |
| 6. | petulant | amiable | grouchy | sullen | peevish |
| 7. | genius | prodigy | wunderkind | average | star |

# Test 37

## A. Synonyms

Select the word that most closely matches the meaning of the word provided.

| | | | | | |
|---|---|---|---|---|---|
| 1. | BONANZA | drop | combine | branch off | windfall | deficit |
| 2. | CLAIRVOYANT | psychic | unaware | peevish | genial | clueless |
| 3. | DEPLORABLE | great | wretched | disintegrate | clamp | admirable |
| 4. | ELATION | gloom | creative writing | leaflet | joy | despair |
| 5. | ANTECEDENT | capricious | ancestor | following | descendant | steadfast |

## B. Fill in the Blanks

Fill in the blanks from the words in the table below. There is one extra word you do not need.

| daunting | nosegay | struggle | banal | vexed | palatable |
|---|---|---|---|---|---|

1. The bride carried a small _____ of roses on her wedding day.

2. The students found the history lecture to be _____ and boring, struggling to stay awake during class.

3. Although the challenge was _____, the team worked together and achieved their goal.

4. The dish that was served at the school lunch was not very _____, causing many students to refuse to eat it.

5. The child was _____ by the math problem, unable to solve it.

## C. Antonyms

Pick the word that means the opposite or near opposite of the word provided.

| | | | | | |
|---|---|---|---|---|---|
| 1. | AKIN | promulgate | unlike | alike | same | similar |
| 2. | FETTER | chain | recalcitrant | freedom | contemptable | bond |
| 3. | SNIDE | pleasant | sarcastic | idolatrous | nasty | fanatical |
| 4. | JOCULAR | witty | aficionado | serious | fervent | comical |
| 5. | MALTREAT | mistreat | collocation | temperance | mollycoddle | abuse |

## D. Homophones and Homographs

Homophones are two or more words having the same pronunciation but different spellings and meanings. Homographs are words which have the same spelling but different meanings.

From the list below, fill in the blanks.

| not | leased | naught | knot | least |
|---|---|---|---|---|

1.  The athlete's performance was a complete _____, as he failed to score a single point.

2.  Party unity is threatened when members will _____ compromise.

3.  At _____ I'll be able to relax and get some rest on the weekend.

4.  Parts of the building are _____ out to tenants.

5.  I tied the rope in a tight _____ to make sure it wouldn't come undone.

# Test 38

## A. Synonyms

Select the word that most closely matches the meaning of the word provided.

| | | | | | |
|---|---|---|---|---|---|
| 1. | FEROCIOUS | gentle | pickpocket | placid | divest | savage |
| 2. | GIDDY | steady | boon | dizzy | milieu | stable |
| 3. | HURTLE | crawl | rush | fading | go slowly | nascent |
| 4. | INIMICAL | affable | unfriendly | frontrunner | hazy | agreeable |
| 5. | JOCUND | hail | hemorrhage | merry | despondent | blue |

## B. Sentence Completion - Double Blanks

Select the correct answer from the options provided.

1. A healthy diet includes a balance of _____ and _____.

A) fiber...protein          B) junk...sweet          C) fast food...candies          D) honey...frozen food

2. Despite being very _____, he struggled to _____ the test.

A) smart...fail          B) intelligent...pass          C) injudicious...write          D) imprudent...do

3. There is no _____ for laziness in the _____ sector.

A) tolerance...corporate          B) bigotry...workplace          C) excuse...languor          D) room...sloth

4. Although fun to play with, _____ should be handled with _____.

A) rocks...reckless          B) reptiles...neglect          C) bikes...stress          D) fireworks...care

## C. Analogies

Select the correct answer from the options provided.

1   SIEVE is to FLOUR as
A) blender is to salt
B) juicer is to meat
C) whisk is to fruits
D) tongs are to milk
E) strainer is to pasta

2   COOKING is to STOVE as
A) rewind is to fast forward
B) skating is to rink
C) pleased is to satisfied
D) highway is to turnpike
E) school is to studying

3   FATIGUE is to SLEEP DEPRIVATION as
A) thirst is to dehydration
B) fever is to vertigo
C) dizziness is to hot
D) headache is to backache
E) nausea is to cold

4   EXACERBATE is to DETERIORATE as
A) support is to undermine
B) optimism is to nihilism
C) ameliorate is to improve
D) prosper is to shrivel
E) chassis is to transmission

## D. Similar Words - Odd One Out
Mark the word that is NOT similar to the other words.

| | | | | | |
|---|---|---|---|---|---|
| 1. | profusion | scarcity | opulence | copiousness | abundance |
| 2. | proficiency | prowess | dexterity | incompetence | expertise |
| 3. | raze | obliterate | rebuild | wreck | wipe out |
| 4. | abdicate | embrace | repudiate | renounce | relinquish |
| 5. | confront | shirk | evade | shun | sidestep |
| 6. | impulsive | calculated | spontaneous | unprompted | intuitive |
| 7. | pristine | tattered | frayed | ragged | dilapidated |

# Test 39

## A. Synonyms

Select the word that most closely matches the meaning of the word provided.

| | | | | | | |
|---|---|---|---|---|---|---|
| 1. | AMBIVALENCE | conviction | indecision | spur | quell | certainty |
| 2. | BANAL | tract | flier | trite | fortification | subdivision |
| 3. | CAPRICIOUS | fickle | stable | alarm | rancor | steady |
| 4. | DELINQUENT | law-abiding | maverick | punctual | hoist | criminal |
| 5. | EMBODIMENT | non-entity | condoned | illness | personification | disorganization |

## B. Fill in the Blanks

Fill in the blanks from the words in the table below. There is one extra word you do not need.

| ungainly | benevolence | catastrophe | adulterate | attenuate | tyrant |
|---|---|---|---|---|---|

1. The turtle was agile in water but _____ on land.

2. The food vendor was arrested for trying to _____ the fruit smoothies with cheap, artificial sweeteners.

3. The volunteer's _____ towards old people was admirable.

4. The scientist used a machine to _____ the effects of harmful X-rays.

5. The earthquake was a _____ for the town, causing widespread damage.

## C. Antonyms

Pick the word that means the opposite or near opposite of the word provided.

1. INTROVERT      reclusive     blinker      gregarious    retiring      pabulum

2. INCONVENIENCE  benefit       biddable     nuisance      intransigent  incommode

3. MITIGATE       credence      alleviate    aggravate     hate          attachment

4. ORIENT         perplex       adjust       truss         abjure        align

5. POTENT         impotent      important    strong        mighty        dynamic

## D. Homophones and Homographs

Homophones are two or more words having the same pronunciation but different spellings and meanings. Homographs are words which have the same spelling but different meanings.

From the list below, fill in the blanks.

| suite | cemetery | dessert | symmetry | sweet |
|-------|----------|---------|----------|-------|

1. For _____, there's apple pie, cheesecake, and fruit.

2. Guests were invited to the publisher's hospitality _____ to meet the author.

3. The _____ was a peaceful and somber place, with rows of graves and headstones.

4. The pudding was so _____ that I couldn't resist having another slice.

5. Classical dance in its purest form requires _____ and balance.

# Test 40

## A. Synonyms

Select the word that most closely matches the meaning of the word provided.

| | | | | | |
|---|---|---|---|---|---|
| 1. | ESPIONAGE | honesty | reassurance | counted | transparency | spying |
| 2. | FIRMAMENT | ground | gauzy | acute | heavens | abyss |
| 3. | GOSSAMER | robust | enthrone | delicate | divest | thick |
| 4. | HAUGHTINESS | modesty | disinherit | meekness | acquiesce | arrogance |
| 5. | NEGATE | refute | mellow | affirm | fretful | confirm |

## B. Sentence Completion - Double Blanks

Select the correct answer from the options provided.

1. Although _____, riding on a motorbike should be done with _____.

A) enjoyable...responsibility    B) frustrating...neglect    C) fun...carelessness    D) vexing...desertion

2. The writer has a _____ sense of storytelling. His novels are always _____ with interesting plots and characters.

A) strong...laden    B) weak...filled    C) poor...shown    D) remarkable...lacking

3. Individuals who have undergone difficult and _____ job _____ often end up developing negative feelings toward work.

A) cheerful...days    B) jovial...hours    C) joyful...time    D) stressful...experiences

4. It is important to _____ your personal space and _____ the privacy of others.

A) protect...invade    B) defend...intrude    C) cherish...respect    D) have...violate

## C. Analogies

Select the correct answer from the options provided.

| | |
|---|---|
| 1   FLUTTER is to TREMBLE as | 2   INTANGIBLE is to TOUCH as |
| A)   twitch is to throw | A)   visible is to see |
| B)   shudder is to shake | B)   fervid is to heat |
| C)   jolt is to bolt | C)   cough is to smell |
| D)   pulsate is to jest | D)   inaudible is to listen |
| E)   jump is to fall | E)   luminous is to light |
| | |
| 3   BRITTLE is to BREAK as | 4   PAINTINGS are to FRAME as |
| A)   solid is to evaporate | A)   books are to table |
| B)   rigid is to bend | B)   museum is to ocean |
| C)   elastic is to stretch | C)   page is to paper |
| D)   malleable is to snap | D)   restaurant is to desert |
| E)   sturdy is to blow | E)   statues are to pedestal |

## D. Similar Words - Odd One Out
Mark the word that is NOT similar to the other words.

| | | | | | |
|---|---|---|---|---|---|
| 1. | torrid | sweltering | sultry | frigid | scorching |
| 2. | usurp | seize | relinquish | arrogate | commandeer |
| 3. | lively | vigorous | vivacious | stolid | spirited |
| 4. | meretricious | false | legitimate | specious | deceptive |
| 5. | lewd | coarse | refined | bawdy | vulgar |
| 6. | inveterate | occasional | confirmed | habitual | chronic |
| 7. | innate | intrinsic | inborn | learned | inherent |

# Test 41

## A. Synonyms

Select the word that most closely matches the meaning of the word provided.

1. AVID            apathetic      devoted        grouchy       indifferent     breezy

2. BRAVADO         modesty        exultant       boldness      disconsolate    cowardice

3. CONCILIATORY    pacifying      changeless     picky         antagonistic    provocative

4. DESOLATION      cheer          misery         joy           painstaking     bliss

5. EMULATE         imitate        spurn          ignore        reject          neglect

## B. Fill in the Blanks

Fill in the blanks from the words in the table below.  There is one extra word you do not need.

| demure | tread | sequential | judgment | astute | beguile |
|--------|-------|------------|----------|--------|---------|

1. The new girl was very _____, rarely speaking up in class.

2. The teacher taught the lessons in a _____ manner, starting with the basics.

3. The soldier was careful to _____ lightly as he walked through the minefield.

4. The _____ detective solved the difficult case, using all the clues at her disposal.

5. The charming salesman was able to _____ the customer into buying the overpriced product.

## C. Antonyms

Pick the word that means the opposite or near opposite of the word provided.

| | | | | | | |
|---|---|---|---|---|---|---|
| 1. | BANISH | eject | invite | profligacy | exile | ban |
| 2. | APLOMB | assurance | aspersion | awkwardness | depredation | composure |
| 3. | CAUTERIZE | besot | burn | mensch | singe | extinguish |
| 4. | MOOR | tie | pother | berth | poise | unknot |
| 5. | PERVASIVE | localized | prevalent | censor | rife | widespread |

## D. Homophones and Homographs

Homophones are two or more words having the same pronunciation but different spellings and meanings. Homographs are words which have the same spelling but different meanings.

From the list below, fill in the blanks.

| peon | mowed | bank | paean | mode |
|---|---|---|---|---|

1.   The song is a _____ to solitude and independence.

2.   In some contexts, the term _____ can be used in a derogatory or demeaning way.

3.   The lawn was freshly _____, the grass trimmed and neat.

4.   The shares were underwritten by the _____ of England.

5.   The company claimed to have identified a _____ of contamination for the vaccine.

# Test 42

## A. Synonyms

Select the word that most closely matches the meaning of the word provided.

1. FERVENT      apathetic      vault      disburse      impassioned      indifferent

2. GARRULOUS      reserved      chatty      cleave      cold      accumulate

3. HIEMAL      wintry      amalgamate      baking      abscond      summery

4. LAX      tight      correspond      coincide      taut      loose

5. MAUDLIN      impassive      stoic      apathetic      sentimental      blight


## B. Sentence Completion - Double Blanks

Select the correct answer from the options provided.

1. Despite being extremely _____, she was _____ at the party.

A) sad...joyful          B) alone...funny          C) down...quite          D) popular...alone


2. People who are _____ can _____ their living spaces neat.

A) messy...maintain          B) tidy...disorganize          C) organized...keep          D) cluttered...hold


3. The _____ chef not only cooked classic dishes but also created new _____ recipes on his own.

A) experienced...innovative      B) old...skillful          C) new...poisonous          D) practiced...unsavory

4. They could only rescue a few animals from the _____ after it was destroyed by a _____ fire.

A) zoo...raging          B) ground...mild          C) room...slight          D) wild...minor

## C. Analogies

Select the correct answer from the options provided.

1   DISHEVELED is to COMB as
A)  foul is to dirty
B)  ghoulish is to sleazy
C)  broken is to sterile
D)  wrinkled is to iron
E)  salubrious is to attired

2   BATTERY is to FLASHLIGHT as
A)  letter is to word
B)  needle is to wheedle
C)  screw is to nail
D)  bird is to beak
E)  kitchen is to cup

3   EASEL is to ARTIST as
A)  musician is to mic
B)  chisel is to doctor
C)  stethoscope is to sculptor
D)  solider is to weapon
E)  podium is to speaker

4   FLIMSY is to UNSUBSTANTIAL as
A)  inadequate is to insufficient
B)  abundant is to disappointing
C)  sturdy is to study
D)  dodgy is to honest
E)  circuitous is to straight

## D. Similar Words - Odd One Out
Mark the word that is NOT similar to the other words.

| | | | | | |
|---|---|---|---|---|---|
| 1. | woe | anguish | despair | glee | distress |
| 2. | longing | urge | compulsion | plan | impulse |
| 3. | justification | absolution | conviction | exoneration | vindication |
| 4. | brave | gutless | valiant | intrepid | gallant |
| 5. | taint | defilement | purity | contamination | stain |
| 6. | substantial | significant | considerable | trivial | ample |
| 7. | soprano | shrill | treble | bass | high-pitched |

# Test 43

## A. Synonyms

Select the word that most closely matches the meaning of the word provided.

1. ADIEU          howdy       hello           welcome       deadpan      farewell

2. BERSERK        composed    crazy           humility      sane         pellucid

3. CANTANKEROUS   crabby      good-natured    courage       pleasant     audacity

4. DIMINUTION     progress    seethe          cyst          decrease     growth

5. ECLECTIC       narrow      diverse         simmer down   fume         specific

## B. Fill in the Blanks

Fill in the blanks from the words in the table below. There is one extra word you do not need.

| fanaticism | objector | engulfed | emancipate | discursive | disembark |
|------------|----------|----------|------------|------------|-----------|

1. The tourists had to _____ from the bus and walk the rest of the way to the attraction due to ongoing construction on the road.

2. The small town was _____ by the forest fire.

3. The politician's supporters showed _____ towards their candidate.

4. She moved abroad as she thought that was the only way to _____ herself from her past.

5. The speaker's presentation was _____, going off on tangents rather than staying on topic.

## C. Antonyms

Pick the word that means the opposite or near opposite of the word provided.

| | | | | | |
|---|---|---|---|---|---|
| 1. | PETRIFY | reassure | impregnate | nullify | frighten | terrify |
| 2. | NEBULOUS | precise | vague | indistinct | catheterize | hazy |
| 3. | EXPERIENCED | crafty | stupid | expert | cunning | inexperienced |
| 4. | APPARITIONAL | ghostly | acrimony | flummox | spectral | tangible |
| 5. | INNOCUOUS | innocent | offensive | ruined | kindly | safe |

## D. Homophones and Homographs

Homophones are two or more words having the same pronunciation but different spellings and meanings. Homographs are words which have the same spelling but different meanings.

From the list below, fill in the blanks.

| ceiling | leach | spring | sealing | leech |
|---|---|---|---|---|

1.  A _____ is a type of worm-like creature that feeds on the blood of animals.

2.  He was a bibliophile, and the books in his room were stacked from floor to _____.

3.  _____ food in an airtight jar starves the bacteria of oxygen and they are unable to reproduce.

4.  Nitrates _____ from the soil into rivers.

5.  The _____ fashion trends are all about bright colors and bold patterns.

# Test 44

## A. Synonyms

Select the word that most closely matches the meaning of the word provided.

| | | | | | |
|---|---|---|---|---|---|
| 1. | FLIRTATIOUS | kittenish | serious | mortuary | sober | appealing |
| 2. | GROTESQUE | ugly | centralize | beautiful | forked | fitting |
| 3. | HOMOGENIZE | separate | distinguish | classy | standardize | furor |
| 4. | IMPISH | obedient | divest | roguish | serious | docile |
| 5. | LUDICROUS | sensible | ridiculous | refurbish | confiscate | mindful |

## B. Sentence Completion - Double Blanks

Select the correct answer from the options provided.

1. The school should provide pupils with _____ exchange programs to help them learn about different cultures and _____.

A) cultural...traditions    B) community...couture    C) services...tribes    D) racial...vernacular

2. The local community center offers _____ for kids to learn new _____ and skills.

A) classes...jobs    B) seminars...courses    C) workshops...hobbies    D) knacks...flairs

3. Many young people are interested in environmental _____ and are _____ to learn more about it.

A) conservation...eager    B) destruction...droopy    C) collapse...apathetic    D) devastation...weary

4. The math problem _____ the students, causing them to _____.

A) informed...neglect    B) consuming...run    C) educated...sleep    D) stumped...give up

## C. Analogies

Select the correct answer from the options provided.

1  ATLAS is to MAPS as
A)  engine is to frame
B)  gazetteer is to geography
C)  ocean is to creek
D)  brain is to cranium
E)  law is to statute

2  CULTIVATE is to NEGLECT as
A)  nurture is to disregard
B)  plain is to simple
C)  fissure is to crack
D)  develop is to expound
E)  kindle is to rouse

3  LEGUME is to BEAN as
A)  radio is to podcast
B)  kitchen is to sink
C)  human is to bones
D)  sweet is to sour
E)  fish is to cod

4  MUTE is to SOUND as
A)  drive is to stay
B)  sleep is to exercise
C)  quiet is to noise
D)  hear is to speak
E)  scream is to tranquil

## D. Similar Words - Odd One Out
Mark the word that is NOT similar to the other words.

| | | | | | |
|---|---|---|---|---|---|
| 1. | sleek | streamlined | jagged | smooth | glossy |
| 2. | shroud | veil | blanket | expose | wrap |
| 3. | iniquity | immorality | heinousness | virtue | vice |
| 4. | reprove | criticize | endorse | chastise | rebuke |
| 5. | reimburse | deduct | return | compensate | indemnify |
| 6. | affluent | impoverished | prosperous | abounding | booming |
| 7. | infuriate | exasperate | calm | enrage | rile |

# Test 45

## A. Synonyms

Select the word that most closely matches the meaning of the word provided.

| | | | | | | |
|---|---|---|---|---|---|---|
| 1. | OBFUSCATE | clarify | fuse | confuse | earmark | elucidate |
| 2. | PARSIMONIOUS | cheap | countermand | extravagant | retract | decadent |
| 3. | EXORBITANT | reasonable | deprecate | plume | extortionate | rational |
| 4. | CORRODE | strengthen | cloud | eat away | approval | fortify |
| 5. | ASPERSION | applause | slander | dilly-dally | temporize | appreciation |

## B. Fill in the Blanks

Fill in the blanks from the words in the table below. There is one extra word you do not need.

| acquittal | upheaval | confounded | indolent | boisterous | spearhead |
|---|---|---|---|---|---|

1. The puzzle _____ the solver, causing frustration.

2. The leader of the scouting group decided to _____ the search for a new campsite.

3. The students at the school were upset by the _____ of their usual routine when the teachers went on strike.

4. The _____ of the famous actor was met with cheers and applause in the courtroom.

5. The party was _____, with loud music and peppy guests.

## C. Antonyms

Pick the word that means the opposite or near opposite of the word provided.

| | | | | | |
|---|---|---|---|---|---|
| 1. | FORTIFY | weaken | armaments | antipode | cusp | munitions |
| 2. | SPOOF | vivid | straggle | biped | honesty | parody |
| 3. | DETRIMENTAL | beneficial | negative | breach | splice | injurious |
| 4. | MUNIFICENT | bountiful | zenith | miserly | nadir | liberal |
| 5. | PERTURB | soothe | agitate | pessimistic | adverse | ruffle |

## D. Homophones and Homographs

Homophones are two or more words having the same pronunciation but different spellings and meanings. Homographs are words which have the same spelling but different meanings.

From the list below, fill in the blanks.

| ingenious | trip | ingenuous | deprecate | depreciate |
|---|---|---|---|---|

1.   The children will not respect you if you constantly _____ them.

2.   Shares continued to _____ on the stock markets today.

3.   The _____ calls for careful advance planning.

4.   The inventor's solution to the problem was so _____ that it won first prize in the competition.

5.   Jessica's _____ nature made her an easy target for the con man.

# Test 46

## A. Synonyms

Select the word that most closely matches the meaning of the word provided.

1. SINISTER      baleful      vital      trace      summery      amble

2. EXIGENT      trivial      flower      urgent      achromatic      minor

3. DESTITUTE      prosperous      penniless      smash      delay      affluent

4. EROSION      wearing away      buildup      object      harmonize      strengthening

5. IMPRESSIONABLE      vaporize      proof      susceptible      transpire      impervious

## B. Sentence Completion - Double Blanks

Select the correct answer from the options provided.

1. Many parents are _____ about the lack of mental health resources in the school system and are _____ for change.

A) talking...ignoring      B) concerned...advocating      C) quiet...admitting      D) silent...vocalizing

2. The city council is _____ adding outdoor fitness equipment to the public parks to _____ more physical activity.

A) considering...encourage      B) flaunting...daunt      C) trying...suppress      D) ignore...discourage

3. The complex text _____ the reader, _____ them to lose interest.

A) bewildered...causing      B) clarified...making      C) elucidated...having      D) illustrated...effecting

4. My friend was _____ about her finances, so we sat down and brainstormed some potential _____.

A) talking...problems      B) unconcerned...snags      C) carefree...results      D) worried...solutions

## C. Analogies

Select the correct answer from the options provided.

1   SPACECRAFT is to SPACE as
A)   navy is to shipman
B)   alpine is to resort
C)   mart is to grocery
D)   elevator is to building
E)   shell is to peanut

2   SHELF is to BOOK as
A)   banana is to peel
B)   ewe is to ram
C)   barista is to coffee shop
D)   rainfall is to drowning
E)   drawer is to clothing

3   SPORADIC is to INFREQUENT as
A)   discern is to oversight
B)   welcome is to repudiate
C)   persistent is to consistent
D)   grow is to shrink
E)   persuade is to dissuade

4   CALLIGRAPHY is to INK as
A)   crocheting is to thread
B)   sketching is to portraits
C)   reading is to knowledge
D)   running is to athletics
E)   jamming is to music

## D. Similar Words - Odd One Out
Mark the word that is NOT similar to the other words.

| | | | | | |
|---|---|---|---|---|---|
| 1. | precipice | crag | baffle | cliff | escarpment |
| 2. | impersonator | inventor | forger | imitator | plagiarist |
| 3. | mendacity | honesty | perjury | fabrication | spuriousness |
| 4. | orchestrate | ignore | coordinate | arrange | plan |
| 5. | pernicious | noxious | innocuous | toxic | lethal |
| 6. | puzzle | confound | bewilder | explicate | mystify |
| 7. | beggar | mendicant | vagabond | prosperous | panhandler |

# Test 47

## A. Synonyms

Select the word that most closely matches the meaning of the word provided.

| | | | | | |
|---|---|---|---|---|---|
| 1. | LUSCIOUS | distasteful | eventuate | delicious | perish | dry |
| 2. | MISANTHROPE | humanitarian | synchronize | pessimist | antedate | philanthropist |
| 3. | OASIS | haven | contemporize | barren | preexist | droughty |
| 4. | PARTAKE | participate | indolent | abstain | zealous | refrain |
| 5. | QUIESCENT | inactive | vigorous | spatial | temporal | energetic |

## B. Fill in the Blanks

Fill in the blanks from the words in the table below. There is one extra word you do not need.

| deciduous | jovial | applaud | immutable | bemoaned | accustomed |
|---|---|---|---|---|---|

1. The _____ trees in the forest lose their leaves every fall and grow new ones in the spring.

2. Although many things in life are subject to change, some values and beliefs are considered _____ and remain constant throughout one's lifetime.

3. The host was in a _____ mood, making everyone feel welcome.

4. After living in a cold climate for many years, I have become _____ to wearing warm clothes and gloves during the winter.

5. The musician _____ the loss of his instrument, expressing sadness.

## C. Antonyms

Pick the word that means the opposite or near opposite of the word provided.

| | | | | | |
|---|---|---|---|---|---|
| 1. | PALPABLE | obvious | plain | evident | soufflé | intangible |
| 2. | NEGATE | affirm | glorious | refute | counter | cancel |
| 3. | KILN | furnace | expatiate | icebox | impervious | oven |
| 4. | CACOPHONY | tarmac | dissonance | asphalt | harmony | discord |
| 5. | BUOYANT | morose | slayer | upbeat | antecedent | cheery |

## D. Homophones and Homographs

Homophones are two or more words having the same pronunciation but different spellings and meanings. Homographs are words which have the same spelling but different meanings.

From the list below, fill in the blanks.

| finance | gambol | gamble | horde | hoard |
|---|---|---|---|---|

1. Her publishers knew they were taking a _____ when they agreed to publish such an unusual novel.

2. Digging in her garden, she uncovered a _____ of gold dating back to the 9th century.

3. The _____ department is responsible for managing the company's financial affairs.

4. The young dogs like to play and _____ about.

5. The _____ of zombies shambled toward the survivors, their moans and groans filling the air.

# Test 48

## A. Synonyms

Select the word that most closely matches the meaning of the word provided.

1.  RIGOROUS    lax     strict     repast     intercede     lenient

2.  ARTIFICE    sincerity     trickery     snail     highflier     honesty

3.  BLEAK    jovial     plush     exigent     depressing     cheery

4.  SQUEAMISH    fastidious     perturb     laidback     incite     easygoing

5.  INDECENT    proper     fruition     impolite     decorous     covert

## B. Sentence Completion - Double Blanks

Select the correct answer from the options provided.

1. There is no _____ for dishonesty in the _____.

A) room...zoo     B) space...library     C) lenience...courtyard     D) tolerance...courtroom

2. The community is concerned about the _____ in the river and is calling for stricter

_____.

A) smog...disorders     B) litter...breach     C) pollution...regulations     D) trash...results

3. Many _____ in the city complain that house prices are too high and not _____.

A) residents...affordable     B) township...expensive     C) people...luxurious     D) inhabitants...costly

4. The _____ 's work contributed to a number of important scientific _____ in the field of genetics.

A) chef...findings     B) scientist...discoveries     C) expert...recipes     D) professor...failures

## C. Analogies

Select the correct answer from the options provided.

1   OVERWORK is to BURNOUT as
A)   boost is to diminish
B)   depression is to hopelessness
C)   process is to complicate
D)   reinforce is to undercut
E)   brood is to elation

2   FOSTER is to HINDER as
A)   clarify is to confuse
B)   malign is to defame
C)   disconnect is to eliminate
D)   naive is to simple
E)   assuage is to allay

3   GASKET is to ENGINE as
A)   stove is to burner
B)   phone is to screen
C)   door is to handle
D)   bulb is to filament
E)   rotor is to turbine

4   SADNESS is to DESPAIR as
A)   elation is to anguish
B)   content is to affliction
C)   misfortune is to jubilation
D)   guilt is to remorse
E)   desolation is to euphoria

## D. Similar Words - Odd One Out
Mark the word that is NOT similar to the other words.

| | | | | | |
|---|---|---|---|---|---|
| 1. | inane | intelligent | absurd | crass | frivolous |
| 2. | imbue | drain | permeate | infuse | fill |
| 3. | tittle-tattle | truth | rumor | gossip | hearsay |
| 4. | glib | shallow | profound | facile | superficial |
| 5. | gawk | ignore | scowl | gape | stare |
| 6. | foolhardy | rational | hotheaded | reckless | hasty |
| 7. | succeeding | preceding | ensuing | subsequent | following |

# Test 49

## A. Synonyms

Select the word that most closely matches the meaning of the word provided.

1. DISGRUNTLED    satisfied    resentful    gratified    entreaty    exultant

2. CONTORT    uniform    undeform    distort    align    petition

3. COHABIT    part    scatter    disperse    co-reside    befit

4. ABASE    demean    demand    respect    counter    admiration

5. LUGUBRIOUS    blithe    doleful    diverse    didactic    jubilant

## B. Fill in the Blanks

Fill in the blanks from the words in the table below. There is one extra word you do not need.

| inauspicious | obsessive | evacuate | etiquette | hiatus | fleeting |
|---|---|---|---|---|---|

1. During his _____ from work, he traveled to several exotic countries and had many exciting adventures.

2. Despite the _____ beginning, the team managed to pull off an impressive win.

3. The summer heat was _____, and soon the leaves began to turn yellow and fall from the trees.

4. He was a/an _____ collector of rare stamps and spent hours each day searching for new additions to his collection.

5. In case of a fire, it is important to _____ the building immediately and call for help.

## C. Antonyms

Pick the word that means the opposite or near opposite of the word provided.

| | | | | | |
|---|---|---|---|---|---|
| 1. | OBSTRUCT | hinder | bar | facilitate | essential | thwart |
| 2. | NONPARTISAN | biased | scam | neutral | clank | nonaligned |
| 3. | MANDATORY | fixed | encumber | toll | obligatory | optional |
| 4. | JADED | fatigued | impede | fresh | basket | wearied |
| 5. | INEXPLICABLE | complicated | outdid | unshakable | knotty | explicable |

## D. Homophones and Homographs

Homophones are two or more words having the same pronunciation but different spellings and meanings. Homographs are words which have the same spelling but different meanings.

From the list below, fill in the blanks.

| graphed | mourning | incense | graft | morning |
|---|---|---|---|---|

1.  _____ burned in the corner of the office.

2.  The family was in _____ for a month.

3.  The global warming data will be _____, and the students will interpret it.

4.  I always have a cup of coffee in the _____ to help wake me up.

5.  His administration was marked by widespread _____ and crime.

# Test 50

## A. Synonyms

Select the word that most closely matches the meaning of the word provided.

| | | | | | |
|---|---|---|---|---|---|
| 1. | PENULTIMATE | foremost | sheep | second last | radical | initial |
| 2. | RATIFY | reject | recycled | privilege | discard | sanction |
| 3. | PROCURE | abandon | acquire | strange | forsake | lose |
| 4. | PRESUMPTUOUS | undue | preview | modest | discreet | impudent |
| 5. | OBVIATE | permit | continue | avoid | allot | allow |

## B. Sentence Completion - Double Blanks

Select the correct answer from the options provided.

1. The farmer had to _____ the hay into the barn before the _____ storm hit.

A) bring...impending     B) done...passed     C) pass...ebbing     D) make...receding

2. Despite the _____ funding and resources, the team of scientists was able to make a _____ breakthrough in their research.

A) pitiable...close     B) lowly...near     C) excellent...crushing     D) inadequate...huge

3. The company's _____ financial planning resulted in a _____ success in the market.

A) meager...fine     B) major...trivial     C) outstanding...significant     D) poor...major

4. Despite the _____ of the task, she remained focused and completed it with _____ and determination.

A) simplicity...inaccuracy     B) unfussiness...neglect     C) ease...carelessness     D) difficulty...hard work

## C. Analogies

Select the correct answer from the options provided.

1  COMPASS is to NAVIGATING as
A) barrier is to separation
B) delighted is to revel
C) binoculars are to birdwatching
D) musician is to microphone
E) teacher is to classroom

2  QUILLS are to INKWELL as
A) refrigerator is to ice
B) keys are to keyboard
C) nails are to hammer
D) microwave is to food
E) chip is to forest

3  MUDDY is to RINSE as
A) competition is to compete
B) mountain is to hill
C) splintered is to glue
D) glimmer is to shimmer
E) snowstorm is to blizzard

4  BEAR is to SALMON as
A) horse is to carp
B) scientist is to experiments
C) dog is to leash
D) toad is to grub
E) lynx is to wolf

## D. Similar Words - Odd One Out
Mark the word that is NOT similar to the other words.

| | | | | | |
|---|---|---|---|---|---|
| 1. | confiscate | commandeer | restore | sequester | impound |
| 2. | growth | rust | decay | erosion | corrosion |
| 3. | fade | wane | wax | decrease | decline |
| 4. | vicious | malevolent | rancorous | gentle | venomous |
| 5. | sell | hawk | vend | buy | peddle |
| 6. | mayhem | turmoil | tranquility | commotion | chaos |
| 7. | inertia | torpor | compassion | indolence | lethargy |

# Answers and Explanations

## Test 1

### A. Synonyms

1. indirect          2. incriminate          3. flexible          4. ruler          5. honest

### B. Fill in the Blanks

1. recuperate          2. legible          3. jubilation          4. disclose          5. synopsis

### C. Antonyms

1. love          2. joined          3. weakness          4. decrease          5. arrogance

### D. Homophones and Homographs

1. flower          2. reign          3. mail          4. flour          5. rain

## Test 2

### A. Synonyms

1. trusting          2. fear          3. seeing          4. enthusiast          5. elaborate

### B. Double Blanks

1. B          2. C          3. B          4. A

### C. Analogies

1. A- the heart pumps blood throughout the body, similar to how the lungs bring oxygen to the body. The other options do not have the same relationship.
2. D- you sleep on a bed and work on a desk. Object-activity relationship.
3. E- a key is used to unlock things, such as doors or locks, similar to how a pen is used to write.
4. C- a book contains information, similar to how a phone is used for communication.

### D. Similar Words - Odd One Out

1. anger          2. optimist          3. apathy          4. suppress          5. accept

6. clear          7. fake

# Test 3

## A. Synonyms

1. talkative        2. fanatic        3. paradise        4. temporary        5. insult

## B. Fill in the Blanks

1. toxic        2. sustain        3. upright        4. abide        5. vindictive

## C. Antonyms

1. close        2. uphold        3. surplus        4. provide        5. wither

## D. Homophones and Homographs

1. bear        2. bare        3. cell        4. cel        5. sell


# Test 4

## A. Synonyms

1. irresponsible        2. enemy        3. rough        4. lonely        5. dry out

## B. Double Blanks

1. C        2. A        3. A        4. D

## C. Analogies

1. A- both pairs of words are synonyms with the same grammatical structures.
2. C- both pairs of words have the same degree of intensity.
3. E- both pairs of words are antonyms with the same grammatical structures.
4. D- they both have the same grammatical structures and similar desirable forms of quality.

## D. Similar Words - Odd One Out

1. rescued        2. deprive        3. repel        4. naive        5. inadvertent

6. divine        7. gloomy

## Test 5

### A. Synonyms

1. honest       2. insignificant       3. trailblazer       4. encourage       5. intolerant

### B. Fill in the Blanks

1. aroma       2. ghastly       3. biased       4. bounty       5. distinguished

### C. Antonyms

1. amity       2. belittle       3. yielding       4. soiled       5. illicit

### D. Homophones and Homographs

1. road       2. barking       3. dye       4. rode       5. die


## Test 6

### A. Synonyms

1. mortal       2. dulcet       3. compel       4. overlook       5. shun

### B. Double Blanks

1. C       2. B       3. D       4. A

### C. Analogies

1. D- both pairs of words share an increase in the degree of intensity, other options do not have this relationship.
2. B- both share a similar activity: place relation, i.e., swimming is done in water, and skiing is done on snow. Other options do not share this relationship.
3. A- the answers have the same degree of intensity and have the same grammatical structures.
4. D- they both share cause and effect relation, whereas the other answers do not.

### D. Similar Words - Odd One Out

1. gradual       2. incoherent       3. shut       4. punctually       5. disgrace

6. repress       7. hesitant

# Test 7

## A. Synonyms

1. alluring     2. adverse     3. incriminate     4. juvenile     5. placid

## B. Fill in the Blanks

1. pungent     2. flicker     3. trauma     4. vacant     5. aligned

## C. Antonyms

1. add     2. calm     3. assertive     4. stimulating     5. normal

## D. Homophones and Homographs

1. claque     2. hare     3. clack     4. hair     5. sail

# Test 8

## A. Synonyms

1. endure     2. adaptable     3. lofty     4. averse     5. loathe

## B. Double Blanks

1. C     2. D     3. A     4. B

## C. Analogies

1. E- they both share the performer and object relationship, while others do not.
2. A- both pairs of words work in a similar way, and perform a specific function. Other options do not have this relationship.
3. C- in this case, characteristic qualities are being compared that are positively related, other options do not have this relationship.
4. D- they both have the same classification relation, which the other options do not possess.

## D. Similar Words - Odd One Out

1. save     2. aspiration     3. virtuous     4. fragmented     5. meager

6. judicious     7. tactful

## Test 9

### A. Synonyms

1. commanding     2. fracas     3. listlessness     4. impairment     5. comparison

### B. Fill in the Blanks

1. thriving     2. abolish     3. malicious     4. chorus     5. blossom

### C. Antonyms

1. junk     2. disperse     3. venom     4. experienced     5. benign

### D. Homophones and Homographs

1. look     2. knight     3. meat     4. night     5. meet

## Test 10

### A. Synonyms

1. wanderer     2. traditional     3. ironic     4. exposed     5. dictator

### B. Double Blanks

1. C     2. A     3. D     4. A

### C. Analogies

1. B- they both share a similar degree and form of quality.
2. A- both pairs of words are antonyms with the same grammatical structures.
3. B- both pairs of words are synonyms with the same grammatical structures.
4. C- they both are the vocalizations of different types of animals and the different sounds they make, whereas some other answers do not have this relationship.

### D. Similar Words - Odd One Out

1. ardent     2. violation     3. circumspect     4. ignorant     5. commoner

6. backfire     7. notorious

# Test 11

## A. Synonyms

1. flexibility    2. folly    3. strengthen    4. covert    5. noisy

## B. Fill in the Blanks

1. berth    2. chameleon    3. disparity    4. encroach    5. dabble

## C. Antonyms

1. disbelief    2. belittle    3. introduce    4. withhold    5. dart

## D. Homophones and Homographs

1. complement    2. batter    3. compliment    4. cede    5. seeds


# Test 12

## A. Synonyms

1. ignoble    2. frantic    3. aghast    4. excise    5. astonish

## B. Double Blanks

1. C    2. B    3. A    4. B

## C. Analogies

1. D- both pairs of words have a part-to-whole relationship, whereas the other options do not share this connection.
2. A- they both have the correct location relationship, which the other options lack.
3. E- both pairs of words have the action: object relationship, which the other answers do not have.
4. C- they both share the correct performance: performer relation, whereas the other options do not share this connection.

## D. Similar Words - Odd One Out

1. certainty    2. knack    3. bizarre    4. diverse    5. daunt

6. fundamental    7. assurance

## Test 13

### A. Synonyms

1. iniquitous    2. diaphanous    3. gloomy    4. grasp    5. cling

### B. Fill in the Blanks

1. equilibrium    2. facilitate    3. figurative    4. grovel    5. aesthetic

### C. Antonyms

1. unafraid    2. normality    3. dispossess    4. authentic    5. lazy

### D. Homophones and Homographs

1. peace    2. auricle    3. piece    4. sentence    5. oracle


## Test 14

### A. Synonyms

1. diminish    2. belligerent    3. succumb    4. discredit    5. era

### B. Double Blanks

1. A    2. C    3. A    4. D

### C. Analogies

1.  D- they both show an increase in intensity. The other options do not have the same relationship.
2.  B- they both have the action-subject relationship, which the other options lack.
3.  E- taxonomy is a system of classification for organizing, and hierarchy is a system of ranking or organizing things in order of importance or status. Other options do not have similar structures.
4.  A- they both have the object-user relation. The other options do not have the same relationship.

### D. Similar Words - Odd One Out

1. diligent    2. insignificance    3. flourish    4. zest    5. pacify

6. be still    7. elucidate

# Test 15

## A. Synonyms

1. turmoil     2. contrasted     3. drab     4. ploy     5. infuriate

## B. Fill in the Blanks

1. acoustics     2. quart     3. rebuke     4. predominant     5. adage

## C. Antonyms

1. dispassionate     2. undermine     3. be still     4. kind     5. enthusiastic

## D. Homophones and Homographs

1. quires     2. choirs     3. loon     4. palm     5. lune

# Test 16

## A. Synonyms

1. agitator     2. phony     3. cordon     4. yesteryear     5. nauseous

## B. Double Blanks

1. B     2. A     3. D     4. B

## C. Analogies

1. B- they are both synonyms of the respective words. The other options do not have the same relationship.
2. A- both options show a desirable/undesirable form of a quality and are also synonymous.
3. C- they are both logically connected as gardening is done with plants, on a smaller scale, and similarly, farming is done with crops on a larger scale.
4. E- they both have the performer: object relationship, which the other answers do not have.

## D. Similar Words - Odd One Out

1. extravagant     2. shrink     3. loyalist     4. incompetent     5. create

6. bore     7. novice

# Test 17

## A. Synonyms

1. renounce      2. contradict      3. false report      4. obsolete      5. enthusiasm

## B. Fill in the Blanks

1. refutation      2. brusque      3. amiss      4. scathing      5. consolidate

## C. Antonyms

1. reject      2. clever      3. fleeting      4. modest      5. seriousness

## D. Homophones and Homographs

1. threw      2. recede      3. drop      4. through      5. reseed

# Test 18

## A. Synonyms

1. eulogize      2. stimulate      3. thin      4. access      5. courageous

## B. Double Blanks

1. A      2. C      3. C      4. D

## C. Analogies

1. A- the answers are antonyms with the same grammatical structures.
2. C- they both have a part-to-whole relationship, whereas the other options do not share this connection.
3. B- these options share the effect: cause relation, which the other options lack.
4. A- the first word represents a characteristic, while the second represents its corresponding measure or expression. Other options do not have this relation.

## D. Similar Words - Odd One Out

1. substandard      2. compliment      3. gentle      4. tranquil      5. unwilling

6. separate      7. demand

# Test 19

## A. Synonyms

1. insuperable　　2. apathetic　　3. judge　　4. link　　5. incalculable

## B. Fill in the Blanks

1. retribution　　2. sermon　　3. unscathed　　4. ample　　5. passionate

## C. Antonyms

1. ominous　　2. genius　　3. reckless　　4. respected　　5. cheerful

## D. Homophones and Homographs

1. bail　　2. bale　　3. assistance　　4. bark　　5. assistant


# Test 20

## A. Synonyms

1. penurious　　2. arrogant　　3. joke　　4. minor　　5. wobbly

## B. Double Blanks

1. B　　2. A　　3. C　　4. D

## C. Analogies

1. E- they both share a similar increase in intensity.
2. B- both of them share an action: place relation, something the other options lack.
3. D- appease and pacify both involve actions intended to calm or placate, while anger and violence both represent things that can be lessened through these actions.
4. C- they both have action: object relationship. The other options do not have the same relationship.

## D. Similar Words - Odd One Out

1. sterile　　2. commendable　　3. obsolete　　4. gleeful　　5. solid

6. allowance　　7. apparent

## Test 21

### A. Synonyms

1. depravity          2. honor          3. indefinite          4. triumphant          5. delicacy

### B. Fill in the Blanks

1. entourage          2. drizzle          3. craven          4. baleful          5. portentous

### C. Antonyms

1. douse          2. disputable          3. restrained          4. shy          5. quiet

### D. Homophones and Homographs

1. kernel          2. patience          3. colonel          4. well          5. patients


## Test 22

### A. Synonyms

1. insolence          2. diligent          3. crooked          4. deepened          5. benevolent

### B. Double Blanks

1. B          2. D          3. A          4. B

### C. Analogies

1. C- the relation between these pairs of words is that they both involve the use of a specific material to create an item. The other options do not have the same relationship.
2. D - they both involve the use of a specific ingredient or decoration to enhance the appearance or flavor, whereas the other options do not share this connection.
3. A- they both involve the study of specific processes or phenomena. The other options do not have an accurate connection.
4. E- they both share the correct relation in terms of the form of a quality they represent. The other options do not have the same relationship.

### D. Similar Words - Odd One Out

1. stationary          2. scalding          3. callousness          4. consecutively          5. taut

6. thwarted          7. bold

# Test 23

## A. Synonyms

| | | | | |
|---|---|---|---|---|
| 1. fizzy | 2. crush | 3. payment | 4. meticulous | 5. padding |

## B. Fill in the Blanks

| | | | | |
|---|---|---|---|---|
| 1. squabbling | 2. vandal | 3. tactician | 4. parsimonious | 5. pompous |

## C. Antonyms

| | | | | |
|---|---|---|---|---|
| 1. stiff | 2. odorless | 3. negligent | 4. damning | 5. acquired |

## D. Homophones and Homographs

| | | | | |
|---|---|---|---|---|
| 1. ring | 2. council | 3. gorilla | 4. counsel | 5. guerrilla |

# Test 24

## A. Synonyms

| | | | | |
|---|---|---|---|---|
| 1. captivating | 2. daring | 3. mayhem | 4. aimless | 5. parody |

## B. Double Blanks

| | | | |
|---|---|---|---|
| 1. B | 2. A | 3. D | 4. B |

## C. Analogies

1. E- both pairs of words are synonymous, with the same grammatical structures.
2. D- the first word represents a characteristic, while the second represents its corresponding measure or expression. Other options do not have this relation.
3. A- they both have a correct object: user connection. The other options do not have the same relationship.
4. B- both pairs of words have an accurate example: category relation. The other options do not have the same connection.

## D. Similar Words - Odd One Out

| | | | | |
|---|---|---|---|---|
| 1. ignore | 2. integration | 3. spontaneous | 4. reprimand | 5. zenith |
| 6. belt up | 7. resist | | | |

## Test 25

### A. Synonyms

| 1. appalling | 2. quarrelsome | 3. rebuke | 4. specious | 5. glow |
|---|---|---|---|---|

### B. Fill in the Blanks

| 1. implored | 2. accentuate | 3. coalesce | 4. depleted | 5. hawser |
|---|---|---|---|---|

### C. Antonyms

| 1. tedious | 2. surge | 3. indistinct | 4. simple | 5. reject |
|---|---|---|---|---|

### D. Homophones and Homographs

| 1. marshal | 2. principal | 3. martial | 4. principle | 5. match |
|---|---|---|---|---|

## Test 26

### A. Synonyms

| 1. grimace | 2. mindless | 3. move | 4. suppress | 5. reserve |
|---|---|---|---|---|

### B. Double Blanks

| 1. A | 2. A | 3. D | 4. C |
|---|---|---|---|

### C. Analogies

1. B- they both have the correct action-object relationship, which the other options lack.
2. B- both pairs of words show an increase in the intensity of the particular objects. This relation is absent in other options.
3. C- these pairs of words correctly depict an action and the resulting outcome. The other options do not have the same relationship.
4. A- both pairs of words are antonyms with the same grammatical structures.

### D. Similar Words - Odd One Out

| 1. refuge | 2. denial | 3. deface | 4. run | 5. waver |
|---|---|---|---|---|

| 6. degrade | 7. deliberate |
|---|---|

# Test 27

## A. Synonyms

| | | | | |
|---|---|---|---|---|
| 1. compensation | 2. variegated | 3. spike | 4. revitalized | 5. prolific |

## B. Fill in the Blanks

| | | | | |
|---|---|---|---|---|
| 1. abscond | 2. bimonthly | 3. fatuous | 4. gargantuan | 5. callous |

## C. Antonyms

| | | | | |
|---|---|---|---|---|
| 1. hideous | 2. harmony | 3. consistency | 4. shed | 5. glance |

## D. Homophones and Homographs

| | | | | |
|---|---|---|---|---|
| 1. phase | 2. gene | 3. faze | 4. jean | 5. bass |


# Test 28

## A. Synonyms

| | | | | |
|---|---|---|---|---|
| 1. cringe | 2. model | 3. companionship | 4. stronghold | 5. define |

## B. Double Blanks

| | | | |
|---|---|---|---|
| 1. A | 2. C | 3. A | 4. C |

## C. Analogies

1. D- they both have an object: user relationship. A submarine is a type of vessel used by the navy, and a subway is a type of transportation system used by the public.
2. E- both pairs of words are units used for measurement. Other options have incorrect relations.
3. B- both pairs of words correctly relate to the art and the material that is used in the process. The other options do not have the same relationship.
4. C- both pairs of words show a decrease in the intensity of the event. This relation is absent in other options.

## D. Similar Words - Odd One Out

| | | | | |
|---|---|---|---|---|
| 1. thriving | 2. serious | 3. expose | 4. striking | 5. inhibition |
| 6. welfare | 7. reverent | | | |

# Test 29

## A. Synonyms

| 1. recognized | 2. contradict | 3. whim | 4. thin | 5. imperfect |

## B. Fill in the Blanks

| 1. deleterious | 2. egregious | 3. harrowing | 4. imprudent | 5. lucid |

## C. Antonyms

| 1. inept | 2. confidence | 3. similar | 4. diffident | 5. discourage |

## D. Homophones and Homographs

| 1. faint | 2. waive | 3. wave | 4. cast | 5. feinted |


# Test 30

## A. Synonyms

| 1. hopeless | 2. refined | 3. endanger | 4. suspicious | 5. diverge |

## B. Double Blanks

| 1. B | 2. C | 3. A | 4. D |

## C. Analogies

1. A- they both have the correct action: outcome relationship, which the other options lack.
2. C- both pairs of words have the object: storage connection. This relation is absent in other options.
3. D- these pairs of words have a correct action and location relation. The other options do not have the same connection.
4. B- both pairs of words have a correct cause-and-effect connection, which the other options lack.

## D. Similar Words - Odd One Out

| 1. convinced | 2. facilitate | 3. restricted | 4. honesty | 5. purify |
| 6. foe | 7. selfishness |

# Test 31

## A. Synonyms

| 1. crest | 2. inferior | 3. implicit | 4. omnipresent | 5. fluency |
|----------|-------------|-------------|----------------|------------|

## B. Fill in the Blanks

| 1. zealous | 2. woeful | 3. vacillate | 4. sedentary | 5. ruminate |
|------------|-----------|--------------|--------------|-------------|

## C. Antonyms

| 1. wealthy | 2. delight | 3. boorish | 4. reality | 5. poor |
|------------|------------|------------|------------|---------|

## D. Homophones and Homographs

| 1. groan | 2. grease | 3. grown | 4. Greece | 5. content |
|----------|-----------|----------|-----------|------------|


# Test 32

## A. Synonyms

| 1. onlooker | 2. float | 3. passionate | 4. shy | 5. whimper |
|-------------|----------|---------------|--------|------------|

## B. Double Blanks

| 1. B | 2. B | 3. A | 4. A |
|------|------|------|------|

## C. Analogies

1. D- these pairs of words have an object: function, which the other options lack.
2. D- both pairs of words depict a part-whole relationship.
3. E- in these pairs of words, the first words are parts of the second words. The other options do not have the same relationship.
4. A- both pairs of words are synonyms with the same grammatical structures.

## D. Similar Words - Odd One Out

| 1. happy | 2. fluke | 3. furtive | 4. participant | 5. approving |
|----------|----------|------------|----------------|--------------|

| 6. punish | 7. ineptitude |
|-----------|---------------|

# Test 33

## A. Synonyms

| 1. clumsy | 2. guarded | 3. porous | 4. greedy | 5. shrewdness |

## B. Fill in the Blanks

| 1. peculiar | 2. obedience | 3. latitude | 4. furl | 5. mischievous |

## C. Antonyms

| 1. finite | 2. profane | 3. closing | 4. disperse | 5. decent |

## D. Homophones and Homographs

| 1. affection | 2. canon | 3. cannon | 4. affectation | 5. interest |


# Test 34

## A. Synonyms

| 1. lethal | 2. torture | 3. covert | 4. blameworthy | 5. impede |

## B. Double Blanks

| 1. C | 2. A | 3. D | 4. B |

## C. Analogies

1. C- both pairs of words are antonyms with the same grammatical structures.
2. A- both pairs of words correctly show the function of particular senses. This relation is absent in other options.
3. E- these pairs of words correctly relate to the particular emotions and are synonymous. The other options do not have the same relationship.
4. B- both pairs of words have a correct part: whole relationship, with the same grammatical structures.

## D. Similar Words - Odd One Out

| 1. chirpy | 2. incarceration | 3. lucidity | 4. optimism | 5. bore |

| 6. enrage | 7. precise |

# Test 35

## A. Synonyms

1. greed          2. recuperation          3. disclose          4. pleasure seeker          5. ominous

## B. Fill in the Blanks

1. regal          2. dogmatic          3. criterion          4. enthusiasm          5. masquerade

## C. Antonyms

1. dull          2. fill          3. stay          4. communicative          5. wake

## D. Homophones and Homographs

1. site          2. cite          3. our          4. sight          5. hour


# Test 36

## A. Synonyms

1. obstinate          2. cancerous          3. showy          4. prevent          5. soaked

## B. Double Blanks

1. C          2. B          3. A          4. D

## C. Analogies

1. E- they both have the action: subject relationship, which the other options lack.
2. E- the first word represents a characteristic, while the second represents its corresponding measure or expression. Other options do not have this relation.
3. B- these pairs of words correctly relate to the families of the particular animals. The other options do not have the correct relationship.
4. A- both pairs of words have the correct instrument: subject area relationship with the same grammatical structures.

## D. Similar Words - Odd One Out

1. conservatism          2. submissive          3. discernable          4. listener          5. comfort

6. amiable          7. average

# Test 37

### A. Synonyms

1. windfall     2. psychic     3. wretched     4. joy     5. ancestor

### B. Fill in the Blanks

1. nosegay     2. banal     3. daunting     4. palatable     5. vexed

### C. Antonyms

1. unlike     2. freedom     3. pleasant     4. serious     5. mollycoddle

### D. Homophones and Homographs

1. naught     2. not     3. least     4. leased     5. knot

# Test 38

### A. Synonyms

1. savage     2. dizzy     3. rush     4. unfriendly     5. merry

### B. Double Blanks

1. A     2. B     3. A     4. D

### C. Analogies

1. E- both pairs of words correctly show the function of objects. This relation is absent in other options.
2. B- both pairs of words have a correct action and object/place relation.
3. A- both pairs of words have a correct cause-and-effect connection, sleep deprivation causes fatigue, and dehydration causes thirst.
4. C- both pairs of words are synonyms with the same grammatical structures.

### D. Similar Words - Odd One Out

1. scarcity     2. incompetence     3. rebuild     4. embrace     5. confront

6. calculated     7. pristine

# Test 39

## A. Synonyms

1. indecision    2. trite    3. fickle    4. criminal    5. personification

## B. Fill in the Blanks

1. ungainly    2. adulterate    3. benevolence    4. attenuate    5. catastrophe

## C. Antonyms

1. gregarious    2. benefit    3. aggravate    4. perplex    5. impotent

## D. Homophones and Homographs

1. dessert    2. suite    3. cemetery    4. sweet    5. symmetry


# Test 40

## A. Synonyms

1. spying    2. heavens    3. delicate    4. arrogance    5. refute

## B. Double Blanks

1. A    2. A    3. D    4. C

## C. Analogies

1.  B- both flutter and shudder correctly describe an increase in the intensity of movements or vibrations for tremble and shake. The other options do not have the same relationship.
2.  D- the first words in these pairs have a quality that cannot be touched or heard by that particular sense. This relation is absent in other options.
3.  C- these pairs of words correctly relate to the characteristics of materials that are related to their strength or flexibility.
4.  E- both pairs of words have a correct object and place relationship, unlike the other options.

## D. Similar Words- Odd One Out

1. frigid    2. relinquish    3. stolid    4. legitimate    5. refined

6. occasional    7. learned

## Test 41

### A. Synonyms

| 1. devoted | 2. boldness | 3. pacifying | 4. misery | 5. imitate |

### B. Fill in the Blanks

| 1. demure | 2. sequential | 3. tread | 4. astute | 5. beguile |

### C. Antonyms

| 1. invite | 2. awkwardness | 3. extinguish | 4. unknot | 5. localized |

### D. Homophones and Homographs

| 1. paean | 2. peon | 3. mowed | 4. bank | 5. mode |

## Test 42

### A. Synonyms

| 1. impassioned | 2. chatty | 3. wintry | 4. loose | 5. sentimental |

### B. Double Blanks

| 1. D | 2. C | 3. A | 4. A |

### C. Analogies

1. D- both disheveled and wrinkled describe qualities or characteristics that are not smooth or orderly, while comb and iron describe how to fix them. Other options do not have this relation.
2. A- both pairs of words have a correct part: whole relation, which is missing in the other options.
3. E- these pairs of words correctly present an object: user relation. The other options do not have the same connection.
4. A- both pairs of words are synonyms with the same grammatical structures.

### D. Similar Words - Odd One Out

| 1. glee | 2. plan | 3. conviction | 4. gutless | 5. purity |
| 6. trivial | 7. bass |

# Test 43

## A. Synonyms

1. farewell        2. crazy        3. crabby        4. decrease        5. diverse

## B. Fill in the Blanks

1. disembark       2. engulfed     3. fanaticism    4. emancipate     5. discursive

## C. Antonyms

1. reassure        2. precise      3. inexperienced 4. tangible       5. offensive

## D. Homophones and Homographs

1. leech           2. ceiling      3. sealing       4. leach          5. spring


# Test 44

## A. Synonyms

1. kittenish       2. ugly         3. standardize   4. roguish        5. ridiculous

## B. Double Blanks

1. A               2. C            3. A             4. D

## C. Analogies

1. B- an atlas is a book of maps; a gazetteer is a reference book that provides information about geography. Other options do not have this relation.
2. A- both pairs of words are antonyms with the same grammatical structures.
3. E- bean is a type of legume while cod is a type of fish.
4. C- both pairs of words share a correct action: object relation. The other options lack this connection.

## D. Similar Words - Odd One Out

1. jagged          2. expose       3. virtue        4. endorse        5. deduct

6. impoverished    7. calm

# Test 45

## A. Synonyms

1. confuse    2. cheap    3. extortionate    4. eat away    5. slander

## B. Fill in the Blanks

1. confounded    2. spearhead    3. upheaval    4. acquittal    5. boisterous

## C. Antonyms

1. weaken    2. honesty    3. beneficial    4. miserly    5. soothe

## D. Homophones and Homographs

1. deprecate    2. depreciate    3. trip    4. ingenious    5. ingenuous


# Test 46

## A. Synonyms

1. baleful    2. urgent    3. penniless    4. wearing away    5. susceptible

## B. Double Blanks

1. B    2. A    3. A    4. D

## C. Analogies

1. D- they both have the correct object-location relationship, as spacecraft is used to move in space while an elevator is used to move in buildings.
2. E- both pairs of words show a correct storage place for the particular objects. This relation is absent in other options.
3. C- both pairs of words are synonyms with the same grammatical structures.
4. A- these pairs of words correctly relate an action and material involved in the process. The other options do not have the same relationship.

## D. Similar Words - Odd One Out

1. baffle    2. inventor    3. honesty    4. ignore    5. innocuous

6. explicate    7. prosperous

# Test 47

## A. Synonyms

| 1. delicious | 2. pessimist | 3. haven | 4. participate | 5. inactive |

## B. Fill in the Blanks

| 1. deciduous | 2. immutable | 3. jovial | 4. accustomed | 5. bemoaned |

## C. Antonyms

| 1. intangible | 2. affirm | 3. icebox | 4. harmony | 5. morose |

## D. Homophones and Homographs

| 1. gamble | 2. hoard | 3. finance | 4. gambol | 5. horde |


# Test 48

## A. Synonyms

| 1. strict | 2. trickery | 3. depressing | 4. fastidious | 5. impolite |

## B. Double Blanks

| 1. D | 2. C | 3. A | 4. B |

## C. Analogies

1.  B- both pairs of words have a correct cause-and-effect connection, which the other options lack.
2.  A- both pairs of words are antonyms with the same grammatical structures.
3.  E- these pairs of words correctly show a part: whole relationship. The other options do not have the same relationship.
4.  D- these pairs of words correctly relate to the particular emotions and are synonymous. The other options do not have the same relationship.

## D. Similar Words - Odd One Out

| 1. intelligent | 2. drain | 3. truth | 4. profound | 5. ignore |

| 6. rational | 7. preceding |

## Test 49

### A. Synonyms

| | | | | |
|---|---|---|---|---|
| 1. resentful | 2. distort | 3. co-reside | 4. demean | 5. doleful |

### B. Fill in the Blanks

| | | | | |
|---|---|---|---|---|
| 1. hiatus | 2. inauspicious | 3. fleeting | 4. obsessive | 5. evacuate |

### C. Antonyms

| | | | | |
|---|---|---|---|---|
| 1. facilitate | 2. biased | 3. optional | 4. fresh | 5. explicable |

### D. Homophones and Homographs

| | | | | |
|---|---|---|---|---|
| 1. incense | 2. mourning | 3. graphed | 4. morning | 5. graft |

## Test 50

### A. Synonyms

| | | | | |
|---|---|---|---|---|
| 1. second last | 2. sanction | 3. acquire | 4. impudent | 5. avoid |

### B. Double Blanks

| | | | |
|---|---|---|---|
| 1. A | 2. D | 3. C | 4. D |

### C. Analogies

1. C- they both have the object: action relationship, which the other options lack.
2. B- both pairs of words have a correct object: location relationship. This connection is absent in other options.
3. C- both muddy and splintered describe qualities or characteristics that can be fixed through rinse and glue. Other options do not have this relation.
4. D- both pairs of words share a correct hunter: prey relation, which is missing in other options.

### D. Similar Words - Odd One Out

| | | | | |
|---|---|---|---|---|
| 1. restore | 2. growth | 3. wax | 4. gentle | 5. buy |
| 6. tranquility | 7. compassion | | | |

Made in the USA
Las Vegas, NV
08 December 2024

13657486R00072